APPLYING EMOTIONAL INTELLIGENCE

A Practitioner's Guide

edited by

Joseph Ciarrochi
University of Wollongong

John D. Mayer
University of New Hampshire

Psychology Press
Taylor & Francis Group

NEW YORK AND HOVE

Published in 2007
by Psychology Press
270 Madison Avenue
New York, NY 10016
www.psypress.com

Published in Great Britain
by Psychology Press
27 Church Road
Hove, East Sussex BN3 2FA
www.psypress.co.uk

Psychology Press is an imprint of the Taylor & Francis Group, an informa business

Typeset by RefineCatch Limited, Bungay, Suffolk, UK
Printed in the USA by Edwards Brothers, Inc. on acid-free paper
Paperback cover design by Hybert Design

10 9 8 7 6 5 4 3 2 1

Library of Congress Cataloging-in-Publication Data
    Applying emotional intelligence : a practitioner's guide / edited by
Joseph Ciarrochi & John D. Mayer.
        p. cm.
    Includes bibliographical references and index.
    ISBN-13: 978-1-84169-461-0 (hardback : alk. paper)
    ISBN-13: 978-1-84169-462-7 (pbk. : alk. paper)   1. Emotional intelligence.
I. Ciarrochi, Joseph.   II. Mayer, John D., 1953–
    BF576.I47 2007
    152.4—dc22
                                                                2006033852

ISBN: 978-1-84169-461-0 (hbk)
ISBN: 978-1-84169-462-7 (pbk)

CONTENTS

About the Editors   vii
List of Contributors   viii
List of Figures   ix
List of Tables   xi

Introduction   xii

Joseph Ciarrochi and John D. Mayer

1   **Emotional Intelligence in the Classroom: Skill-Based Training for Teachers and Students**   1

Marc A. Brackett and Nicole A. Katulak

2   **Developing Emotional Intelligence Competencies**   28

Richard E. Boyatzis

3   **A Theory-Based, Practical Approach to Emotional Intelligence Training: Ten Ways to Increase Emotional Skills**   53

Susan A. Kornacki and David R. Caruso

4   **Improving Emotional Intelligence: A Guide to Mindfulness-Based Emotional Intelligence Training**   89

Joseph Ciarrochi, John Blackledge, Linda Bilich, and Virginia Bayliss

5   **Personality Function and Personality Change**   125

John D. Mayer

6   **The Key Ingredients of Emotional Intelligence Interventions: Similarities and Differences**   **144**

Joseph Ciarrochi and John D. Mayer

Author Index   **157**

Subject Index   **163**

ABOUT THE EDITORS

Joseph Ciarrochi received his Ph.D. degree from the University of Pittsburgh, a postdoctoral fellowship in emotion research from the University of New South Wales, and currently has a position as lecturer in psychology at the University of Wollongong. He has been conducting cutting-edge research in how emotions influence thinking and behavior and how emotional intelligence can best be measured and used. His findings have been published in the top journals in psychology and have been presented at numerous international conferences. Dr. Ciarrochi is currently evaluating training programs that are designed to increase people's social and emotional intelligence.

John (Jack) D. Mayer received his B.A. degree from the University of Michigan, his M.A. and Ph.D. in psychology at Case Western Reserve University, and then attended Stanford University as a National Institute of Mental Health Post-doctoral Scholar. Dr. Mayer has served on the editorial boards of *Psychological Bulletin* and *Journal of Personality*. He has published numerous scientific articles, book chapters, psychological tests, and books. His articles, with Salovey, in the early 1990s are often credited with beginning research on emotional intelligence.

LIST OF CONTRIBUTORS

Virginia Bayliss
Management and Workplace Programs Continuing Education Directorate, New South Wales Police, Sydney, Australia

Linda Bilich
School of Psychology, University of Wollongong, Australia

John Blackledge
School of Psychology, University of Wollongong, Australia

Richard E. Boyatzis
Department of Organizational Behavior and Psychology, Weatherhead School of Management, Case Western Reserve University, USA

Marc A. Brackett
Department of Psychology, Yale University, USA

David R. Caruso
Department of Psychology, Yale University and EI Skills Group, USA

Joseph Ciarrochi
School of Psychology, University of Wollongong, Australia

Nicole A. Katulak
Department of Psychology, Yale University, USA

Susan A. Kornacki
EI Skills Group, USA

John D. Mayer
Department of Social Psychology/Personality, University of New Hampshire, USA

LIST OF FIGURES

1.1   Perception of Emotion Teacher Activity   8
1.2   Use of Emotion Teacher Activity   10
1.3   Understanding of Emotion Teacher Activity   12
1.4   Management of Emotion Teacher Activity   13
1.5   Perception of Emotion Project: Collage of different facial
      expressions   18
1.6   Use of Emotion Project: Pantene makes you feel . . .?   19
1.7   Understanding of Emotion Project: Real world representa-
      tions of the word "alienation"   21
1.8   Management of Emotion Project: Dealing with anger   22
2.1   Percentage improvement of emotional intelligence from
      behavioral measurement of competencies of different
      groups of MBA graduates taking the Leadership Executive
      Assessment and Development course   33
2.2   Boyatzis' Intentional Change Theory   34
3.1   What would happen to MSCEIT scores after a training
      program?   58
3.2   Mood Meter   61
3.3   Exercise Answer Key   72
3.4   Basic emotions, influence on thinking, level of intensity, and
      facial expression   75
3.5   Emotional lenses   77
3.6   Emotional lenses for Sammy and Maria   78
3.7   Alternative emotional lenses for Sammy and Maria   79
3.8   Emotional Lens Personal Application   81
3.9   Emotional Lens Personal Application: Ideal result   82
4.1   Struggling to get rid of our emotions can be like playing tug
      of war with a monster   99
4.2   Sometimes the best thing to do is let go of the rope   99
4.3   When rules and evaluations are literally believed, they can
      act as prison bars   102
4.4   Here is how a nonverbal creature views your prison   103

4.5   Stars in the sky   106
4.6   The constellation Leo. Our interpretation of the stars   107
4.7   The self-as-context   111
4.8a Struggling to feel special can hurt your relationships. As you
      struggle to be more special, you may make others feel less
      special.   112
4.8b The struggle is an illusion. A nonverbal animal (e.g., a dog)
      would not be able to see the "special" evaluation, or smell it,
      or taste it. The dog would not know what all the fuss is about.   112
4.8c What positive evaluation do you pursue (e.g., "special,"
      "strong," "admirable," "perfect," "attractive")? Write it in the
      balloons.   113
4.9   A visual metaphor of effective action orientation   116
4.10 Valued action often involves many detours and barriers. They
      require one to keep on recommitting to the value   118

LIST OF TABLES

2.1   Intentional Change Theory, the emotional intelligence
development course, and course outputs   36

2.2   Last four years of course evaluations for sections of the
Leadership Executive Assessment and Development course
in the Weatherhead School of Management MBA   39

4.1   Dimensions targeted by Mindfulness-Based Emotional
Intelligence Training (MBEIT) that are hypothesized to
promote emotionally intelligent behavior   98

5.1   A functional analysis of four areas of personality   129–130

5.2   Areas of personality and change goals   140

INTRODUCTION

Joseph Ciarrochi
John D. Mayer

Programs designed to promote social and emotional effectiveness are being tested all over the world, and there is growing evidence for their effectiveness.[1] The central part of this book presents four fascinating interventions in emotional intelligence (EI), developed by some of the most innovative practitioners (and researchers as well, in most instances) side by side. We want you to get a clear sense of what is in the interventions, and how they are similar and different.

We did not want to create yet another EI theory book that describes ideas but provides little that is of direct use to the practitioner. All authors were encouraged to specify, in concrete terms, exactly what was done in their interventions. The book is intended to serve as a guide for future intervention research and for people who would like to engage in EI interventions and make a positive difference in people's lives.

There are many, quite different, approaches to training, coaching, and educating people to improve their personalities in general and emotional intelligence in particular. We have selected four of what we regard as among the best in the area of EI. Some of these programs focus on EI as we would define it; others extend into the far broader terrain of overall personality development.

The four interventions are set up so that readers can appreciate them on their own terms, without evaluation. Then, in the final section of the book, we compare and contrast the interventions, and attempt to identify the key ingredients that are in each intervention; we also discuss personality change more generally. A brief description of the chapters follows.

In Chapter 1, Brackett and Katulak provide a detailed description of a school-based EI intervention. The approach is based on the EI-ability model of Mayer et al.[2] The chapter provides powerful exercises that are designed to improve EI amongst both teachers and students. It also provides useful EI worksheets that help to structure the EI intervention. Finally, the chapter reports preliminary findings on the benefits of the school-based EI intervention for improving well-being, social skills, and grades.

In Chapter 2, Boyatzis presents a broader program for developing personal and interpersonal skills in professionals, managers, and leaders. The program develops personal competencies such as self-awareness, self-management, social awareness, and social management. Using intentional change theory, Boyatzis illustrates how to guide a person through five key life discoveries. The program helps people to clarify their values, and to develop a plan to put these values into play. People are shown how to develop competencies through practice and experiential feedback. The chapter presents longitudinal data suggesting that the Boyatzis EI program can have a long-term impact on people's awareness and management skills.

In Chapter 3, Kornacki and Caruso describe ten ways to improve EI skills in the workplace. The chapter provides a coherent theoretical approach, based on the EI-ability model.[2] It takes readers through a series of case studies to provide concrete illustrations of the EI skills in action. It provides readers with EI assessment and self-development exercises. The intervention is clearly articulated and taught in terms of an Emotional Blueprint, which provides a structured way for people to look at and improve on their emotional experience.

In Chapter 4, Ciarrochi, Blackledge, Bilich, and Bayliss describe a mindfulness-based approach to emotional intelligence training (MBEIT). Unlike other approaches, MBEIT does not teach emotion management skills. Instead, people are taught how to experience their emotions, fully and without defense, and to still do the things they value most. The program focuses on teaching people to let go of unhelpful emotion control strategies, to undermine the power of emotions and thoughts to act as barriers to effective action, and to discover personal values and develop a clear action plan for working toward those values. The program is designed to improve well-being, increase flexibility and effectiveness, and improve interpersonal relationships. The MBEIT approach has received substantial support in the clinical literature and is receiving increasing support within normal populations, in workplace and other settings.

The concluding section of the book contains two chapters that seek to present a unified framework for understanding the wide variety of interventions. In Chapter 5, Mayer presents an overview of personality and of personality change. He divides personality into several areas and discusses change as it relates to each area, the nature of personality change in general (slow, but worth undertaking), and some of the reasons for and goals of change.

In Chapter 6, Ciarrochi and Mayer examine the key ingredients in each of the EI interventions. Some ingredients are shown to be quite similar across interventions. Other ingredients are quite different, and potentially incompatible with each other. The knowns and unknowns about such programs are considered. The end result for the reader, we hope, will be a deeper understanding of EI-related programs, what they do, and how they work.

☐ References

1. Zins, J. E., Bloodworth, M., Weissberg, R. P., & Walberg, H. J. (2006). The scientific base linking social and emotional learning to school success. In J. E. Zins, R. P. Weissberg, M. C. Wang, & H. J. Walberg (Eds.), *Building academic success on social and emotional learning: What does the research say?* (pp. 3–22). New York: Teachers College Press.
2. Mayer, J. D., Salovey, P., & Caruso, D. R. (2004). Emotional intelligence: Theory, findings, and implications. *Psychological Inquiry, 15*, 197–215.

Marc A. Brackett
Nicole A. Katulak

Emotional Intelligence in the Classroom: Skill-Based Training for Teachers and Students

Successful schools ensure that all students master basic skills such as reading and math and have strong backgrounds in other subject areas, including science, history, and foreign language. Recently, however, educators and parents have begun to support a broader educational agenda – one that enhances teachers' and students' social and emotional skills.[1] Research indicates that social and emotional skills are associated with success in many areas of life, including effective teaching, student learning, quality relationships, and academic performance.[2–4] Moreover, a recent meta-analysis of over 300 studies showed that programs designed to enhance social and emotional learning significantly improve students' social and emotional competencies as well as academic performance.[5]

Incorporating social and emotional learning programs into school districts can be challenging, as programs must address a variety of topics in order to be successful.[6,7] One organization, the Collaborative for Academic, Social, and Emotional Learning (CASEL), provides leadership for researchers, educators, and policy makers to advance the science and practice of school-based social and emotional learning programs. According to CASEL, initiatives to integrate programs into schools should include training on social and emotional skills for both teachers and students, and should receive backing from all levels of the district, including the superintendent, school principals, and teachers. Additionally, programs should be field-tested, evidence-based, and founded on sound

1

psychological or educational theory.[6-8] CASEL also recommends that social and emotional learning programs: (1) provide developmentally and culturally appropriate instruction; (2) attempt to create a caring and engaging learning environment; (3) teach children to apply social and emotional skills both in and out of school; (4) enhance school performance by addressing the cognitive, emotional, and social dimensions of learning; (5) encourage family and school partnerships; and (6) include continuous evaluation and improvement.

In this chapter, we describe two programs that fulfill CASEL's requirements and also are compatible with mandates set by *No Child Left Behind* (NCLB),[9] one designed for teachers and the other for middle school students. Both programs are part of a larger initiative involving training and curriculum for school administrators and teachers, parents, and students at all grade levels (i.e., preschool to high school).[10] The programs also are anchored in emotional intelligence (EI) theory,[11] which proposes that four fundamental emotion-related abilities comprise EI, including (1) perception/expression of emotion, (2) use of emotion to facilitate thinking, (3) understanding of emotion, and (4) management of emotion in oneself and others. These four skills promote better quality relationships, enhance emotional health, and improve academic and work performance.[2,3]

The first program is *The Emotionally Intelligent Teacher* (EIT). This full-day workshop, which comes with an activity book, provides teachers of all grade levels with innovative strategies, tools, and techniques to increase their awareness of the importance of EI skills and enhance their ability to employ EI skills in their professional and personal relationships. The second program we describe is *Emotional Literacy in the Middle School* (ELMS). ELMS is a multi-year program that integrates weekly social and emotional learning lessons into existing curricula. There also is a full-day workshop to train teachers on ELMS. Both the EIT and ELMS have been adopted by school districts throughout the United States and abroad, and a comprehensive, multi-method system has been developed to evaluate both programs. Before going into detail about these programs, we provide an overview of EI theory and discuss the importance of emotion-related skills in both teacher and student performance.

☐ Emotional Intelligence

Today, there are two general models of EI in the literature: a skill-based model proposed originally by Mayer and Salovey[11] and a variety of "mixed" approaches.[12-14] According to Mayer and Salovey, EI pertains to an individual's capacity to reason about emotions and to process emotional information to enhance cognitive processes and regulate behavior. For instance, Mayer et al.[15,16] discuss the ability to manage one's own emotions (e.g., the ability to distract oneself temporarily from a difficult situation) as an element of EI. Mixed models, on the other hand, define and measure EI as a set of perceived abilities, skills, and personality traits. For instance, Bar-On's[12] model of EI includes one's perception of his or her ability, "stress tolerance," and basic personality traits such as "optimism." Because both perceived abilities and traits are in the conceptual framework, proponents of the mixed model approach have generally employed self-report measures as opposed to performance measures to assess EI.

Our programs are anchored in the skill-based model of EI. Research indicates that one's estimate of his or her EI (as assessed by self-report as opposed to skill-based measures) is mostly uncorrelated with actual emotion-related ability and does not predict behavior.[17] In our view, keeping EI constrained to a set of emotion-related skills (i.e., the perception, use, understanding, and management of emotion) makes it possible to assess the degree to which EI skills specifically contribute to behavior, as well as provides a firm foundation for developing programs to enhance these skills.[17,18]

The four EI skills included in the Mayer and Salovey[1] model are interrelated, as proficiency in one skill influences mastery in other areas, and cumulative, as mastery on the first three skills culminates in proficiency in the fourth area – management of emotion. Here, we briefly describe the four EI skills; more detailed information can be found elsewhere.[1]

The first skill, *perception of emotion*, refers to the ability to perceive emotions in oneself and others, as well as in other stimuli, including objects, art, stories, and music. The second skill, *use of emotion to facilitate thinking*, refers to the ability to use or generate emotions to focus attention, communicate feelings, or engage in other cognitive processes such as reasoning, problem solving, and decision making. The third skill, *understanding of emotion*, refers to the ability to understand emotional information and the causes of emotions and how emotions combine, progress, and change from one to another. The fourth skill, *management of emotion*, refers to the ability to be open to feelings and employ effective strategies to promote personal understanding and growth.

Mayer and colleagues have developed performance tests of EI, including the Mayer-Salovey-Caruso Emotional Intelligence Tests for adults (MSCEIT)[15] and children (MSCEIT-YV).[19] Both of these tests reliably assess the four-skill model of EI. Moreover, scores on both tests predict a wide range of important life outcomes. Among college students and adults, higher MSCEIT scores are associated with higher quality interpersonal relationships among couples[20] and friends,[21] academic performance and social competence,[17,22] and key workplace outcomes, including stress tolerance and salary.[23] Lower MSCEIT scores are associated with maladaptive behavior, including drug use, alcohol consumption, and fighting.[24,25] Among school children, MSCEIT-YV scores are associated positively with teacher ratings of adaptability, leadership, and study skills and negatively with aggression, anxiety, conduct problems, hyperactivity, and attention and learning problems, as well as self-reported smoking behavior.[26]

The first premise behind our programs is that both teacher and student proficiency in EI is expected to influence effective communication, management of stress and conflict, maintenance of a positive school environment, and academic or workplace success. Teachers experience a wide range of positive and negative emotions while teaching and interacting with students.[4,27] The nature of their job requires dealing with their own emotions as well as those of students, parents, colleagues, and administrators. Moreover, teachers are among the groups displaying the highest levels of occupational stress. In one study, more than 30% of British teachers perceived their jobs as stressful, with reports of increasing pressure.[28] Indeed, stress and poor emotion management continually rank as the primary reasons why teachers become dissatisfied with the profession and end up leaving their positions.[29] There also has been growing alarm at the rate of teacher burnout and the adverse implications this has for the learning environment in schools and the achievement of educational goals.[30] Moreover, teachers who have difficulty regulating their emotions (and their classrooms) tend to have students who experience more negative emotions in class (e.g., sadness, shame, and guilt).[4] We believe that lack of EI skills is one of the roots of these problems and that emotional skills training for teachers can create a more stable, supportive, and productive learning environment – one that encourages positive social interaction, active engagement, and academic achievement among students.

Considerable research indicates that EI skills play a central role in children's academic, personal, and social lives above and beyond the effects of personality and general intelligence. Emotions drive attention,[31] which impacts learning, memory, and behavior. The ability to regulate emotions, for example, can help students to stay focused in class and handle anxiety-arousing situations such as taking tests.[32] Indeed, children with higher EI skills tend to experience higher academic achievement than children with lower EI skills.[22,33–36] It also is possible that some EI skills will interact with intelligence to predict academic achievement, such that children of the same level of intelligence will perform differently in school depending on their level of EI. For example, a highly intelligent student who becomes anxious during a test may fail because he or she has not learned effective strategies to deal with the problem. Thus, providing training in emotion skills may lead to greater academic achievement.[7,37,38] Children with higher EI also tend to behave in more socially appropriate, non-aggressive ways at school and tend to be relatively popular, prosocial, and secure.[39–41] Moreover, deficits in EI skills have been linked to alcohol and tobacco use,[42] anxiety and depression,[43–45] poor physical and psychological health,[46] and violence.[47] For example, the inability to judge emotional expressions in others may be directly associated with hostility and aggression in children, as aggressive children perceive more hostility in others than do non-aggressive children.[48] In contrast, children skilled in the perception of emotion have more positive social interactions.[49] Additionally, children who can express their emotions effectively, both verbally and nonverbally, tend to adhere well to society's rules and norms for communicating how they feel.[36] This is important because students who are able to develop quality social relationships at school feel more comfortable in the school environment, receive better support from teachers and peers, and form healthier attachments to school.[50,51] Thus, we assert that teaching emotional literacy to children is one important way to potentially affect these many aspects of students' lives.

☐ Emotionally Intelligent Teacher Workshop

The goal of the *Emotionally Intelligent Teacher Workshop*[52] is to provide teachers with resources to create a safe, satisfying, caring, and productive school environment. This one-day, highly interactive seminar focuses on leadership and professional development. Because interpersonal relationships have been shown to be a prominent determinant of school effectiveness,[53] another goal is to improve relationships with students and the various stakeholders in the school community.

Tools presented in the workshop are designed to serve as coping mechanisms for stress, which continually ranks as the top reason why teachers leave the profession.[29] Specifically, the workshop provides participants with: (1) in-depth information about the four EI skills (i.e., the perception, use, understanding, and management of emotion), (2) knowledge of how EI skills play an integral role in academic learning, decision making, classroom management, stress management, interpersonal relationships, team building, and the overall quality of one's life, and (3) innovative strategies and tools to increase each EI skill using activities, simulations, and group discussions.

One of the powerful tools offered in the training workshop is the EI Blueprint, a four-question process that helps teachers (and students) deal effectively with emotional experiences such as a meeting with an angry parent or a confrontation with a school bully. The Blueprint integrates scientific theory and practical applications to enhance classroom culture by helping teachers both to prepare for situations they expect to be emotionally difficult as well as to evaluate and cope with emotionally-laden situations they have already encountered. Specifically, it guides teachers to work through these situations using the EI model, skill-by-skill, beginning with perception of emotion and ending with management of emotion.

The Blueprint is a set of four questions that teachers are instructed to ask themselves about an anticipated or past experience. Each question represents one of the four EI skills that the teachers will use in the preparation for, or the evaluation of, the emotional experience. Because emotions contain important information about people and the environment (perception of emotion) and identifying one's own feelings and those of the other person are key factors in how a situation is handled, the first question is "How may/*was* each person feel/*feeling*?" Emotions also influence how we think, and our thoughts influence how we handle a situation (use of emotion). Thus, the second question is, "What may/*were* you and the other person think/*thinking* about as a result of these feelings?" Next, in order to understand the underlying causes of the emotional experience (understanding emotion), teachers ask themselves, "What may cause/*caused* each person to feel the way he/she does/*did*?" The fourth Blueprint question, "What may/*did* you and the other person do to manage these feelings?" deals with the specific strategies that each person uses to handle his or her emotions (management of emotion). This step is vital in planning for and determining the effectiveness of emotional management strategies. The final part of the Blueprint requires participants to reflect on the interaction and write a plan as to how the situation could have been handled more successfully.

Teacher Activities

The EI Teacher Workshop provides teachers with practical activities to do on their own and in their classrooms to further the development of each EI skill. Here we discuss one tool per EI skill; the full set of activities can be found elsewhere.[52] Each activity emphasizes the development of a single EI skill, but practicing one skill will often lead to mastery in other areas of EI as well. The activities are simple exercises that have the potential to foster lifelong skills that are essential for professional and personal success. We encourage routine performance of these exercises or personal variations of them, as well as their application to a variety of contexts inside and outside of work.

Perception of Emotion

The ability to recognize one's own emotions and identify how others are feeling requires attention to multiple internal and external cues and the analysis of both verbal and nonverbal communication in oneself and others. Devoting adequate time and attention to fostering such emotional awareness is extremely important in optimizing teacher effectiveness in multiple domains. For instance, when teachers are able to recognize how they are feeling throughout the day in different situations, they may better express themselves in and out of the classroom. Emotional self-awareness also may help to predict emotions in various circumstances and guide one's behavior. Likewise, the ability to accurately assess the emotions of others can be used to guide the approach a teacher may take to certain lectures and activities, parent–teacher conferences, daily interactions with fellow teachers, and meetings with administrators.

For perception of emotion activity, teachers provide a written description of events that happened over the course of a school day, including what they were doing in these situations and who else was present. Then, they record the emotions they (the teachers) were feeling and the intensity of the emotions during each of these events. Next, they record how they believe those around them were feeling during the same events, including the verbal and nonverbal cues (e.g., facial expressions, voice, posture) that served as a basis for their emotional judgments of these people (see Figure 1.1 for a fill-in sheet for this activity). This activity can be done periodically throughout the day or at the end of the day.

This exercise is designed to: (1) increase the amount of attention one pays to one's own and others' emotions, and (2) enhance one's ability to evaluate the emotions of the self and others. This activity initially requires a pen and paper and time set aside. Over time and with practice, this activity can be modified so that it is done mentally within the teacher's daily routine. Also, to assess the effectiveness of their ability to perceive others' emotions, teachers may choose to ask those around them about their feelings after completing the activity. Teachers can extend this exercise to the other EI skills by adding the following columns to the table: (1) emotions/moods/thoughts generated by the situation and how these were/could be modified, (2) causes of the emotion, and (3) emotion management strategies used, their effectiveness, and other possible strategies.

EVENT/ACTIVITY/ PEOPLE PRESENT	EMOTION/INTENSITY (SELF)	EMOTION CUE/ EMOTION (OTHERS)
EXAMPLE: parent–teacher conference with Billy's mom about Billy's recent grades	EXAMPLE: – somewhat nervous – very cautious – mild compassion	EXAMPLE: – frown: sadness – eyes wide: surprise – leaning forward: interest

FIGURE 1.1. Perception of Emotion Teacher Activity.

Use of Emotion

Because emotions influence the way we think and behave, it is important to be able to use this skill effectively and to be able to generate one's own emotional states as well as those of others in order to establish the appropriate emotional conditions for different types of thinking. Experiencing the right emotions at the right times can improve motivation and energy in the teacher and interest and attention in students. In contrast, certain emotional states experienced in and out of the classroom can be distracting for both students and teachers alike. Similarly, the success of conversations with parents or school administrators is significantly affected by the emotions present during these interactions. For example, attempting to have a focused conversation with someone who is overjoyed about something can be difficult because very positive emotions tends to result in inductive as opposed to deductive reasoning. Hence, teacher effectiveness is dependent upon the abilities to recognize which emotions are best for different situations, to harness emotional energy to facilitate thinking and behavior, and to generate optimal emotional states for different contexts.

For this activity, teachers first write about how certain aspects of their environments affect their emotions, and in turn their motivation, teaching efficacy, and interactions with others. For instance, how do the lighting, music, or other aspects of the settings where they grade papers or teach affect their own and others' emotions and moods? How do these emotions or moods then influence the way they correct papers or their effectiveness in instructing a class? Then, they make a list of what they already do to generate certain moods in themselves or their students. Next, they list different upcoming activities and events for which they would like to put themselves, their students, or others in a certain emotional mindset, such as a specific literature or history lesson. Finally, they list ways they can produce the emotions or moods they are hoping to evoke for each situation; this last part of the activity links to the fourth EI skill, the management of emotion. Some examples of ways to influence emotional states in oneself and others may include different types of lighting, music, emotion-laden readings, mental imagery, or games (see Figure 1.2 for a fill-in sheet for this activity).

The primary goals of this activity are to: (1) increase awareness of how emotions affect the way we think and behave, and (2) develop a set of tools for manipulating the emotions of oneself and others in order to affect thinking, behavior, and especially performance and effectiveness in different domains. This is a great brainstorming activity for teachers to discuss with each other and their students in order to obtain more ideas and feedback. Once a list of potential emotion-generating strategies has been formulated, teachers should try incorporating them into their daily activities and again converse with others to find out what strategies have worked or failed.

Understanding of Emotion

To fully understand oneself and others, one must know what causes emotions and be able to articulate a full range of emotions when describing how oneself or others may be feeling. These skills are particularly relevant in professions such as teaching, which require constant interaction with others and hence a continuous interplay of emotions. For instance, a more confident, outgoing student who volunteers often in class may be relatively unaffected when the teacher says aloud that the answer the student has provided is incorrect. However, the same situation could cause feelings of anxiety, frustration, or embarrassment in a shy or less confident student. In noticing the shy student's reaction, the teacher

MY ENVIRONMENT & ITS EFFECTS ON ME & OTHERS		
EXAMPLE: – After lunch in class on a rainy day, students are tired, bored, and lethargic. – I am tired too, and it is sometimes difficult to be energetic and enthusiastic.		
HOW I GENERATE MOODS IN MYSELF & OTHERS		
EXAMPLE: I sometimes start a lesson with some upbeat music or a joke to get everyone's attention and to bring a little more energy into the room.		
ACTIVITY/EVENT	**DESIRED STATE**	**HOW TO GENERATE**
EXAMPLE: meeting with Susan to discuss her tardiness	EXAMPLE: attentive, patient, calm, firm, compassionate	EXAMPLE: clear mind beforehand with mental imagery

FIGURE 1.2. Use of Emotion Teacher Activity.

may feel guilty and distracted from the lesson. To transform her own and her students' emotions into something more positive, the teacher may decide to discuss the situation and the associated emotions later with the hurt student. This is just one illustration of how a deeper understanding of emotion and an enhanced emotion vocabulary can impact classroom culture, learning, and achievement. However, the ability to understand the triggers of emotions and to communicate about them is essential to the success of all professional and personal relationships.

For this exercise, teachers write about an emotion they or someone they know has felt recently. They write about the intensity of the emotion, how long it lasted, the events that led up to the emotion, how the emotion progressed (e.g. from annoyance to anger to rage), ended, or changed into other emotions, and the events that surrounded the emotion's transformation or departure. Then, they read over what they have written and think about potential causes of the emotion and why they think it changed or went away (see Figure 1.3 for a fill-in sheet for this activity).

The purpose of this activity is for teachers to explore deeply their own and others' emotional experiences in order to: (1) foster a better understanding of the causes of emotions and their progressions, and (2) encourage the use of an advanced emotion vocabulary. The exercise should be repeated periodically with the experience of different types of emotions and situations. It can also be done during or immediately after an emotional experience to facilitate a better understanding of the situation so that it can be dealt with more effectively.

Management of Emotion

The ability to manage emotions in oneself and others is a valuable skill for teachers. Depending on the situation, actively dealing with or distracting oneself from one's own or others' emotions may be more appropriate. Regardless, the frequent implementation of emotion-management strategies is a priceless approach to effective classroom management, stress reduction, functional professional and personal relationships, and overall quality of life. For example, teachers who can manage their own and students' emotions while teaching can create a more open and effective teaching and learning environment with fewer distractions. Similarly, those who can control their emotional reactions and effectively influence how others feel can deal better with difficult conversations with parents and administrators.

For this activity, teachers write about a negative emotion they experience at work, what triggers that emotion, the strategies they have used to deal with that emotion, and how effective each strategy has been. Then, they brainstorm about and record other possible strategies they could implement to manage their negative emotions. For example, self-talk, exercise, talking to a friend or colleague, and deep-breathing are often recommended (see Figure 1.4 for a fill-in sheet for this activity).

The goal of this activity is for teachers to: (1) evaluate the effectiveness of their current strategies for emotion regulation, and (2) explore the

EMOTION/ INTENSITY		
EXAMPLE: *moderate frustration*		
HOW LONG IT LASTED		
EXAMPLE: *most of class period*		
PRECEDING EVENTS		
EXAMPLE: *students passing notes despite my warning*		
EMOTION PROGRESSION		
EXAMPLE: *frustration to anger to guilt to calm*		
EVENTS SURROUNDING EMOTION TRANSFORMATION/ DEPARTURE		
EXAMPLE: *They stopped when I told them I deducted points from their class participation grades.*		
POTENTIAL CAUSES OF INITIAL EMOTION		
EXAMPLE: *I get frustrated when students don't pay attention when I teach.*		
POTENTIAL CAUSES OF EMOTION PROGRESSION		
EXAMPLE: *– Frustration turned to anger as they ignored me.* *– I felt momentarily guilty for deducting points.* *– After thinking more, I thought their actions justified the punishment, and I was calm.*		

FIGURE 1.3. Understanding of Emotion Teacher Activity.

EMOTION		
EXAMPLE: *anxiety*		
TRIGGER		
EXAMPLE: *evaluation by an* *administrator*		
CURRENT/PAST STRATEGIES FOR DEALING WITH EMOTION		
EXAMPLE: *Remind myself of my* *strengths and try to do my* *best and be myself.*		
EFFECTIVENESS OF STRATEGIES USED		
EXAMPLE: *Generally, I feel somewhat* *less anxious.*		
OTHER POSSIBLE STRATEGIES		
EXAMPLE: *– deep breathing* *– plan a lesson I feel more* * comfortable with* *– yoga the morning before* *– take a break for fresh air* * on my free period before* * the evaluation*		

FIGURE 1.4. Management of Emotion Teacher Activity.

possibilities of implementing other approaches to manage their emotions. Teachers can modify the lesson by listing the emotions of their students or others, the strategies they notice others use, and also by listing how they themselves can help those around them manage their emotions more effectively.

Quality Assurance

To ensure successful implementation as well as continuous improvement of the EI Teacher workshop, several steps are taken to evaluate the quality of the program. Sources of program evaluation include a questionnaire distributed to workshop attendees after they have participated, anecdotes from teachers and administrators after they utilize the workshop tools, and follow-up interviews. In general, administrators report improvements in the way they conduct meetings with teachers, fellow administrators, and parents, which they attribute largely to a better understanding of how emotions affect interpersonal relations as well as to their use of the EI Blueprint to plan these meetings.

Classroom teachers report an enhanced ability to consider their own emotional biases and the emotional states of their students when planning lessons or reacting to student behavior. Teachers also describe a heightened awareness of the emotions that students bring with them from home, the playground, or other aspects of their lives in addition to various attempts to account for these emotions in the classroom. For example, instead of rushing directly into schoolwork, one teacher now allows a few minutes first thing in the morning for students to share their feelings. Finally, we are currently designing studies to examine quantifiable changes in EI, work-related stress, and other important outcomes in teachers, other faculty, and administrators as a result of the workshop.

☐ Emotional Literacy in the Middle School

After receiving initial training in the EI Teacher Workshop, teachers are trained in one of our emotional literacy programs for students. The programs are field-tested and provide evidence-based lessons designed to improve academic performance and increase social competence. The programs also are developmentally appropriate (i.e., account for the cognitive, social, and emotional skills of children in different grade levels) and based on EI theory. The primary goal is for students to become *emotionally literate* by gaining a holistic understanding of "feeling" words, which characterize the gamut of human experience such as excitement, shame, alienation, and commitment. In our view, emotional literacy fosters social competence by teaching students self- and social aware-ness, empathy, and healthy communication. Emotional literacy also helps to develop emotion-related skills through the performance of tasks that teach the four fundamental EI skills (i.e., the perception, use, under-standing, and management of emotion). Finally, emotional literacy fosters the key skills emphasized in national educational standards such as NCLB.[9] Specifically, the program promotes overall academic learning by enhancing vocabulary, comprehension, abstract reasoning, creative writing, critical thinking, and problem solving.

Emotional literacy lessons are easily incorporated into traditional school subjects such as language arts and social studies, but can also be taught in other subject areas such as health and science. Given the high demands on teachers, language arts and social studies are the most practical vehicles with which to teach social and emotional skills. Literature and history lessons as well as current events invariably involve characters that experience a myriad of emotional experiences that need to be expressed, understood, and regulated. These characters provide "real world" examples of how emotions play an integral role in human interaction. Finally, the lessons are organized to help teachers to differentiate instruction, thereby supporting the unique and full development of all students.

The majority of our work has taken place in fifth- through eighth-grade classrooms where we have implemented the Emotional Literacy in the Middle School program (ELMS).[54] ELMS provides teachers with six concrete "how to" steps for quick and easy implementation. Each step can be completed in less than 15 minutes or can be extended to the teacher's liking. The steps should be completed in order, with one new feeling word introduced per week. Below is a brief description of the six steps.

1. *Introduction of Feeling Words.* Teachers introduce the feeling word by relating its meaning to students' prior knowledge and personal experiences. For example, before introducing the word "alienation," teachers ask students to talk about a situation in which they felt isolated or as if they did not belong. The first step personalizes the learning experience by helping students to relate to the word both intellectually and emotionally.
2. *Designs and Personified Explanations.* Students then interpret and explain abstract designs in terms of their symbolic representations of feeling words. For example, teachers ask students how a design consisting of several circles separated by a line looks like the word alienation. This step encourages divergent thinking and the visualization of the elements and actions that represent meanings of feeling words.
3. *Academic and Real World Associations.* This step involves students relating feeling words to social issues or academic topics. For example, students are asked to link the word alienation to the 2005 Hurricane Katrina disaster in the USA. This exercise teaches students to evaluate how the people around them and those of different societies and time periods may experience, express, and manage emotions.
4. *Personal Family Association.* Next, students are instructed to have a discussion about the feeling word with a family member at home. For example, students ask parents or other relatives about a time when they felt alienated. This step encourages parental/familial involvement in students' academic work and fosters good communication between children and their families.

5. *Classroom Discussions.* For this step, class discussions are initiated based on student sharing of Academic/Real World Associations and Personal Family Associations. A discussion ensues when the teacher asks other students to respond to their associations or other students' accounts of the situations. For example, in one district, a student discussed how Nelson Mandela was alienated from society in South Africa. This step helps students to expand each other's knowledge base and perspectives through exposure to others' viewpoints.

6. *Creative Writing Assignments.* The final step involves writing assignments using the feeling word of the week. For example, students are asked to write a short story with a beginning, middle, and end about a person who went from being alienated to feeling elated. In this exercise, students incorporate their own ideas and personal experiences into writing and think creatively and critically about how emotions progress and transform in life experiences. This step also provides a means for student expression of a broad range of emotion knowledge.

Student Activities

In addition to the weekly introduction of feeling words through the six steps, there are student activities, which are designed to have students work intensely on certain emotional literacy skills. The activities are brief, teacher-friendly, and easily incorporated into any classroom setting. They go beyond the memory-based learning and logical-abstract thinking that are emphasized in most traditional classroom endeavors. The activities described below are excerpts from the ELMS program; however, they can be tailored to different age groups. For example, for elementary school students, activities and discussions may focus on a single basic emotion (e.g., happiness or anger), whereas for older children, projects may emphasize more subtle or complex emotions (e.g., alienation or hostility) or a range of related emotions (e.g., different levels of sadness, ranging from discontented to forlorn).

We provide a complete description of one sample student activity per EI skill. As you will note, each activity is structured similarly. First, the teacher briefly introduces the activity and the EI skill it is designed to foster. This introduction is followed by the student project itself and concludes with an in-class discussion about the project and its associated EI skill. After initiating the discussion and encouraging the participation of as many students as possible (especially non-volunteers), the teacher should assume a relatively passive role in the discussion. This will encourage more student–student interaction and cooperation.

Perception of Emotion

Children and adults see hundreds of faces throughout the day. These faces express the spectrum of emotions. The ability to accurately identify these emotions can help us to better understand how others feel and to communicate more effectively. Although interpreting nonverbal communications, such as facial expressions, is an essential component to all social interactions, our culture does not explicitly train individuals on these skills. We also rarely receive feedback as to whether we perceive the facial expressions accurately. Thus, the purpose of this project is for students to examine various facial expressions and identify the emotions that they may depict.

Teachers introduce the project with a short description of how people use their voices, different parts of the body, and especially their faces to convey feelings. The teachers explain the importance of knowing how to accurately perceive nonverbal emotional expressions. For example, if someone is displaying a sad facial expression, they may have experienced some kind of loss and be in need of social support. Then, the teacher either describes or shows pictures of a few aspects of the face that may reveal different emotions (e.g., furrowed brows may denote anger; downward turned corners of the mouth may indicate sadness; blushing could be a sign of embarrassment, etc.). Next, the teacher asks students for examples of other aspects of the face that may correspond to different emotions. Students then work individually or in small groups to create a collage or a mobile. During class time or as homework, students peruse the newspaper, comic strips, and magazines to find pictures of faces depicting the expression of a single emotion (e.g., an entire collage of faces depicting happiness), a range of related emotions (e.g., a mobile of faces depicting different levels of anger from annoyed to furious), or a lot of different emotions. Students cut out the pictures and use them to build a collage or mobile.

The finished projects are collected and displayed in the classroom to be presented by the students and discussed as a class (see Figure 1.5). The class discussion should focus on the specific parts of the face, what emotion students think it depicts, and why. Teachers may ask students how the same facial expression may express different emotions or how the same emotion may be expressed in a variety of ways, depending on the person. The conversation may expound on cultural differences in facial expression, other nonverbal emotional expression such as body movement and aspects of the voice, and also why accurate interpretation of nonverbal communication is important.

FIGURE 1.5. Perception of Emotion Project: Collage of different facial expressions.

Use of Emotion

At a young age, most of us are introduced to some form of mass media, and by early childhood, we are well acquainted with many media advertisements. These advertisements are designed to generate particular emotions to make the viewers think a certain way about themselves and the product or service they promote. Because of this, advertisements provide a great medium through which to learn how emotions impact thinking. The purpose of this project is for students to explore how television commercials influence emotions to set the stage for thinking a particular way about themselves and products or services.

Teachers begin with a five-minute introduction on how advertisers often attempt to manipulate our emotions to capture attention and to make us think differently about ourselves and what they are advertising. The teacher either describes or shows a videotape of two or three well-known commercials that evoke emotions (e.g., Campbell's soup commercials evoke happiness, warmth, and peacefulness by showing a smiling mom serving the soup to her cheerful children; Dodge truck commercials evoke confidence and exhilaration with large, muscular men driving fast and fearlessly over rough terrain) and what these emotions are intended to make us think (e.g., mothers who serve Campbell's soup

FIGURE 1.6. Use of Emotion Project: Pantene makes you feel . . .?

are happy and loving; men who drive Dodge trucks are strong and fearless).

The teacher then asks students to think about the emotions or emotional triggers that commercials use and how these emotions may affect their thoughts. Then, students work individually or in small groups to pick a familiar commercial and create a poster depicting the commercial, the audience it targets, its various components used to influence emotions, the emotions it elicits, and the thoughts those emotions may facilitate.

The finished projects are presented by the students and discussed as a class. Figure 1.6 shows a fifth-grade student's project that depicts the emotions she believed Pantene shampoo commercials evoke. The discussion can begin with detailed descriptions of the projects by the students and may continue with a conversation about other times when emotions may affect our thoughts or behavior (e.g., when we are in a good mood, we may be more motivated to clean or do creative types of homework; when in a negative mood, we may be better at critical evaluation such as working through a personal problem or math homework, etc.). Discussions also may include how we may be able to manipulate our own moods to suit different situations (e.g., think of a happy memory to cheer up when feeling down, etc.).

Understanding of Emotion

As children and adults, we often wonder about the underlying causes of our own and others' feelings. All emotions have causes, but they are not always easily identified. One way of developing a better understanding of what causes certain emotions is by analyzing objects, events, people, and situations and then thinking about what emotions they may evoke. The purpose of this project is to think about how different things, people, and places may evoke different emotions.

Teachers introduce the project with a brief description of how emotions have causes, some easier and some more difficult to identify. The teacher either describes two or three circumstances that may cause or have caused particular emotions in the people who experience them (e.g., the birth of a baby causes a mother to be elated; Hurricane Katrina left its victims in states of despair and devastation). The teacher then asks students to think about different experiences and the emotions they trigger. Then, students work individually or in small groups to create a collage. During class time or as homework, students peruse magazines and websites to find pictures of objects, events, people, and situations that may trigger different types of emotions. Students cut out the pictures and use them to build a collage or mobile.

The finished projects are collected and displayed in the classroom to be presented by the students and discussed as a class (see Figure 1.7 for one student's project on the word "Alienated"). Class discussions should focus on the picture, the emotion it elicits, and why it evokes this emotion. Teachers should encourage students to discuss how the same object or situation may trigger different emotions in different people and how an understanding of what causes themselves and others to feel the way they do may benefit them in their relationships with friends and family members.

Management of Emotion

From infancy, we develop different styles of managing the emotions we feel. For instance, newborns turn away from fear-provoking stimuli or suck on pacifiers to decrease their anxiety, toddlers look to their mothers for comfort to reduce feelings of distress, and school-age children begin finding their own tools to regulate frustration or excitement in appropriate ways. Being aware of how we manage our own emotions and those of others is essential to optimal functioning. One way to foster this

FIGURE 1.7. Understanding of Emotion Project: Real world representations of the word "alienation."

awareness is to analyze the ways we handle emotions and the effectiveness of the strategies we use. The purpose of this project is for students to expand their strategies for managing their emotions and to think about which strategies are more effective and why.

For this activity, teachers begin with a short explanation of how people manage their emotions in various ways and how some management strategies are more or less effective than others. The teacher then describes the following: (1) a time when she or someone else (e.g., a family member, friend, character in a book) felt an emotion (e.g., sadness or frustration), (2) what triggered it (e.g., the teacher's daughter, who was learning to ride a bike without training wheels, fell off the bike and skinned her knee), (3) how the emotion was dealt with (e.g., the child cried but then stopped and decided to get back on and try again), (4) what effect the chosen strategy may have had (e.g., the girl eventually learned to ride the bike), and (5) how the emotion could have been managed both more and less effectively (e.g., if the girl had continued crying and not gotten back on the bike, she may never have learned how to ride a bike).

Next, students are asked to think about feeling a particular emotion (the teacher can assign the emotion or let the students choose their own) and different experiences that elicit that emotion. Then, they are asked to write on paper or posterboard (working in class, individually or in groups, or as homework) different ways to effectively handle that emotion. A class discussion is initiated as students are asked to share with the class their posters or the experiences they wrote about and how they managed their emotions. Alternatively, one large poster could be created with the top ten strategies (see Figure 1.8). Class discussions should emphasize as few or as many of the following: what they were feeling, how they reacted, how long the feeling lasted, what or who changed the feeling, how effective that was, and how they may have reacted differently.

Quality Assurance

A comprehensive multi-method system has been developed to evaluate ELMS. First, it is possible to administer various assessments to teachers and students at several time points before, during, and after implementation of the ELMS program. Second, anecdotal feedback is generally collected in meetings between program implementers (or researchers), superintendents, school principals, and teachers. Finally, there is a quality assurance sheet created to monitor teacher adherence to program

FIGURE 1.8. Management of Emotion Project: Dealing with anger.

protocol as well as student and teacher reactions to the program. This sheet is filled out by observers who visit classrooms and observe teachers while they are implementing the program.

Teachers and students exhibit strong, positive reactions to ELMS. According to the teachers, students: (1) seem more comfortable expressing themselves in class without fear of being judged and ridiculed, (2) appear to have a better understanding of their peers and family members, (3) interact more effectively with students with whom they previously were unable to maintain positive interactions, (4) demonstrate less problem behavior and more prosocial behavior, and (5) write better and incorporate feeling words into other curriculum areas. Teachers also report (1) more positive relationships between themselves and other students, (2) more comfort in sharing their own emotions and experiences with their students, (3) a better ability to recognize and respond constructively to students' social and emotional needs, and (4) a keener awareness of their own emotions and how they contribute to maintaining a healthy classroom climate. This is particularly important given research indicating that teachers' emotions influence both teachers' and students' cognitions, motivations, and behavior.[4] Moreover, a recent experiment showed that students who participated in the ELMS program (as compared to the control group) were rated by their teachers as more adaptable, less anxious, depressed, and hyperactive, and as possessing stronger leadership, social, and study skills after just four months of program involvement. Importantly, the students in the ELMS group as compared to the control group also had higher end-of-year grades in reading, writing, and work habits.[26]

☐ Conclusion

In this chapter we have described two ways to infuse EI skills into the classroom. First, we introduced the EI Teacher Workshop. This workshop provides teachers (and other faculty) with a background on the importance of emotions in teaching and learning, an overview of the four EI skills, a set of tools to develop each EI skill, and the Blueprint to help them handle difficult interpersonal situations more effectively.

Second, we discussed ELMS, an emotional literacy program designed to develop emotion-related skills in students. Grounded in EI theory, the program's six steps and supplemental activities focus on the four EI skills: the perception, use, understanding, and management of emotion. The lessons and activities also encourage the use of new vocabulary, abstract and critical thinking, creative writing, and problem-solving skills as well as self- and social awareness, empathy, healthy communication, and student–student interaction. Through these activities, ELMS enhances academic learning and social competence.

Thus far, these programs have been implemented in several schools throughout the United States, including New York, New Jersey, Connecticut, and Arkansas, as well as in districts throughout Kent, England. Feedback from administrators, teachers, parents, and students, as well as preliminary results from our experiments, suggest that the programs are well-received, enjoyable, and producing quantifiable benefits. Teachers and principals report having improved relationships with colleagues, parents, and students. Students report building higher quality relationships with their peers, teachers, and parents. Furthermore, the programs have had a positive impact on school-related performance as well as other personal and school-related outcomes for both students and teachers. We also are currently extending our work to elementary schools[55] as we believe these skills should be introduced as early as possible in life and reinforced continuously throughout development (cf. Ref. 6).

Emotion-related skills play an integral role in people's daily lives.[1,3,5] Incorporating EI training programs into the classroom can result in a number of benefits outside of, but especially within, the academic setting. Indeed, schools that utilize social and emotional learning programs report an increase in academic success, improved quality relationships between teachers and students, and a decrease in problem behavior.[6] This chapter details two such programs designed to benefit students, teachers, and administrators.

☐ Acknowledgments

We would like to thank Marilyn Carpenter, Joseph Ciarrochi, David Caruso, Jack Mayer, Justyna Mojsa, Susan Rivers, Peter Salovey, and Roger Weissberg for their thoughtful input and invaluable feedback on earlier drafts of this chapter. We also would like to thank the 5th and 6th grade teachers at Valley Stream Middle School who shared their ELMS class projects with us for this chapter, as well as Bruce Alster, former principal of the Brooklyn Avenue School and Dr. Edward Fale, Superintendent of Schools, Valley Stream 24.

☐ References

1. Greenberg, M. T., Weissberg, R. P., O'Brien, M. U., Zins, J., Fredericks, L., Resnik, H., & Elias, M. J. (2003). Enhancing school-based prevention and youth development through coordinated social, emotional, and academic learning. *American Psychologist, 58,* 466–474.

2. Brackett, M. A., & Salovey, P. (2004). Measuring emotional intelligence as a mental ability with the Mayer-Salovey-Caruso Emotional Intelligence Test. In G. Geher (Ed.), *Measurement of emotional intelligence* (pp. 179–194). Hauppauge, NY: Nova Science Publishers.

3. Mayer, J. D., Salovey, P., & Caruso, D. (2004). Emotional intelligence: Theory, findings, and implications. *Psychological Inquiry, 15,* 197–215.

4. Sutton, R. E., & Wheatley, K. F. (2003). Teachers' emotions and teaching: A review of the literature and directions for future research. *Educational Psychology Review, 15,* 327–358.

5. Durlak, J. A., & Weissberg, R. P. (2005, August). A major meta-analysis of positive youth development programs. Presentation at the Annual Meeting of the American Psychological Association, Washington, DC.

6. Elias, M., Zins, J., Weissberg, R., Frey, K., Greenberg, T., Haynes, N., Kessler, R., Schwab-Stone, M., & Shriver, T. (1997). *Promoting social and emotional learning: Guidelines for educators.* Alexandria, VA: Association for Supervision and Curriculum Development.

7. Zins, J. E., Weissberg, R. P., Wang, M. C., & Walberg, H. J. (Eds.). (2004). *Building academic success on social and emotional learning.* New York: Teachers College Press.

8. Matthews, G., Zeidner, M., & Roberts, R. D. (2002). *Emotional intelligence: Science and myth.* Cambridge, MA: The MIT Press.

9. *No Child Left Behind Act of 2001* (2001). PL 107–110.

10. Brackett, M. A., Alster, B., Wolfe, C. J., Fale, E., & Katulak, N. A. (in press). Creating an emotionally intelligent school district: A skill-based approach. In R. Bar-On, K. Maree, & M. Elias (Eds.), *Educating people to be emotionally intelligent.* Rondebosch, South Africa: Heinemann.

11. Mayer, J. D., & Salovey, P. (1997). What is emotional intelligence? In P. Salovey & D. Sluyter (Eds.), *Emotional development and emotional intelligence: Educational implications* (pp. 3–34). New York: Basic Books.

12. Bar-On, R. (1997). *BarOn Emotional Quotient Inventory: A measure of emotional intelligence.* Toronto, Canada: Multi-Health Systems.

13. Furnham, A., & Petrides, K. V. (2003). Trait emotional intelligence and happiness. *Social Behavior and Personality, 31,* 815–824.

14. Schutte, N. S., Malouff, J. M., Hall, L. E., Haggerty, D. J., Copper, J. T., Golden, C. J., & Dornheim, L. (1998). Development and validation of a measure of emotional intelligence. *Personality and Individual Differences, 25,* 167–177.

15. Mayer, J. D., Salovey, P., & Caruso, D. (2002). *The Mayer-Salovey-Caruso Emotional Intelligence Test (MSCEIT), Version 2.0.* Toronto, Canada: Multi-Health Systems.

16. Mayer, J. D., Salovey, P., & Caruso, D. (2002). *MSCEIT technical manual.* Toronto, Canada: Multi-Health Systems.

17. Brackett, M. A., Rivers, S., Shiffman, S., Lerner, N., & Salovey, P. (in press). What is the best way to measure emotional intelligence? A case for performance measures. *Journal of Personality and Social Psychology.*

18. Brackett, M. A., & Geher, G. (2006). Measuring emotional intelligence: Paradigmatic shifts and common ground. In J. Ciarrochi, J. P. Forgas, & J. D. Mayer (Eds.), *Emotional intelligence and everyday life* (2nd ed., pp. 27–50). New York: Psychology Press.

19. Mayer, J. D., Salovey, P., & Caruso, D. (2005). *The Mayer-Salovey-Caruso Emotional Intelligence Test – Youth Version (MSCEIT-YV), Research Version 1.0.* Toronto, Canada: Multi-Health Systems.

20. Brackett, M. A., Warner, R. M., & Bosco, J. S. (2005). Emotional intelligence and relationship quality among couples. *Personal Relationships, 12,* 197–212.

21. Lopes, P. N., Brackett, M. A., Nezlek, J. B., Schutz, A., Sellin, I., & Salovey, P. (2004). Emotional intelligence and social interaction. *Personality and Social Psychology Bulletin, 30,* 1018–1034.

22. Gil-Olarte Márquez, P., Palomera Martín, R., & Brackett, M. A. (in press). Relating emotional intelligence to social competence, and academic achievement among high school students. *Psicothema*.

23. Lopes, P. N., Côté, S., Grewal, D., Kadis, J., Gall, M., & Salovey, P. (in press). Emotional intelligence and positive work outcomes. *Psicothema*.

24. Omori, M., Brackett, M. A., Rivers, S., & Salovey, P. (2006). Emotional intelligence, self-esteem, and maladaptive behavior among college students. Unpublished data, Yale University.

25. Brackett, M. A., Mayer, J. D., & Warner, R. M. (2004). Emotional intelligence and its relation to everyday behaviour. *Personality and Individual Differences, 36,* 1387–1402.

26. Brackett, M. A., Rivers, S., & Salovey, P. (2005). Emotional intelligence and its relation to social, emotional, and academic outcomes among adolescents. Unpublished data, Yale University.

27. Hargreaves, A. (1998).The emotional practices of teaching. *Teaching and Teacher Education, 14,* 835–854.

28. Travers, C. J., & Cooper, C. L. (1993). Mental health, job satisfaction and occupational stress among UK teachers. *Work and Stress, 7,* 203–219.

29. Darling-Hammond, L. (2001). The challenge of staffing our schools. *Educational Leadership, 58,* 12–17.

30. Travers, C. J. (2001). Stress in teaching: Past, present and future. In J. Dunham (Ed.), *Stress in the workplace: Past, present and future* (pp. 130–163). Philadelphia, PA: Whurr Publishers.

31. Ohman, A., Flykt, A., & Esteves, F. (2001). Emotion drives attention: Detecting the snake in the grass. *Journal of Experimental Psychology: General, 130,* 466–478.

32. Lopes, P. N., & Salovey, P. (2004). Toward a broader education: Social, emotional, and practical skills. In J. E. Zins, R. P. Weissberg, & H. Walberg (Eds.), *Social and emotional learning and school success* (pp. 76–93). New York: Teachers College Press.

33. Eisenberg, N., Fabes, R. A., Guthrie, I. K., & Reiser, M. (2000). Dispositional emotionality and regulation: Their role in predicting quality of social functioning. *Journal of Personality and Social Psychology, 78,* 136–157.

34. Feldman, R. S., Philippot, P., & Custrini, R. J. (1991). Social competence and nonverbal behavior. In R. S. Feldman & B. Rime (Eds.), *Fundamentals of nonverbal behavior* (pp. 329–350). New York: Cambridge University Press.

35. Halberstadt, A. G., Denham, S. A., & Dunsmore, J. C. (2001). Affective social competence. *Social Development, 10,* 79–119.

36. Saarni, C. (1999). *The development of emotional competence.* New York: The Guilford Press.

37. Salovey, P., & Sluyter, D. J. (1997). *Emotional development and emotional intelligence: Educational implications.* New York: Basic Books.

38. Weissberg, R. P., & Greenberg, M. (1998). School and community competence-enhancement and prevention programs. In W. Damon (Series Ed.) and I. E. Siegel & K. A. Renninger (Vol. Eds.), *Handbook of social psychology: Vol. 4. Child psychology in practice* (5th ed., pp. 877–954). New York: Wiley.

39. Denham, S. A., Blair, K. A., DeMulder, E., Levitas, J., Sawyer, K., Auerbach-Major, S., & Queenan, P. (2003). Preschool emotional competence: Pathway to social competence. *Child Development, 74,* 238–256.

40. Nellum-Williams, R. (1997). Educator's commentary. In P. Salovey & D. Sluyter (Eds.), *Emotional development and emotional intelligence* (p. 164). New York: Basic Books.

41. Rubin, M. M. (1999). *Emotional intelligence and its role in mitigating aggression: A correlational study of the relationship between emotional intelligence and aggression in urban adolescents.* Unpublished Dissertation, Immaculata College, Immaculata, Pennsylvania.

42. Trinidad, D. R., & Johnson, C. A. (2002). The association between emotional intelligence

and early adolescent tobacco and alcohol use. *Personality and Individual Differences, 32,* 95–105.

43. Zeman, J., Shipman, K., & Suveg, C. (2002). Anger and sadness regulation: Predictions to internalizing and externalizing symptoms in children. *Journal of Clinical Child and Adolescent Psychology, 31,* 393–398.

44. Rottenberg, J., Kasch, K. L., Gross, J. J., & Gotlib, I. H. (2002). Sadness and amusement reactivity differentially predict concurrent and prospective functioning in major depressive disorder. *Emotion, 2,* 135–146.

45. Silk, J. S., Steinberg, L., & Morris, A. S. (2003). Adolescents' emotion regulation in daily life: Links to depressive symptoms and problem behaviors. *Child Development, 74,* 1869–1880.

46. Southam-Gerow, M. A., & Kendall, P. C. (2000). A preliminary study of the emotional understanding of youth referred for treatment of anxiety disorders. *Journal of Clinical Child Psychology, 29,* 319–327.

47. Winters, J., Clift, R. J. W., & Dutton, D. G. (2004). An exploratory study of emotional intelligence and domestic abuse. *Journal of Family Violence, 19,* 255–267.

48. Crick, N., & Dodge, K. A. (1994). A review and reformulation of social information-processing mechanisms in children's social adjustment. *Psychological Bulletin, 115,* 74–101.

49. Izard, C., Fine, S., Schultz, D., Mostow, A., Ackerman, B., & Youngstrom, E. (2001). Emotion knowledge as a predictor of social behavior and academic competence in children at risk. *Psychological Science, 12,* 18–23.

50. Agostin, R. M., & Bain, S. K. (1997). Predicting early school success with development and social skills screeners. *Psychology in the Schools, 34,* 219–228.

51. O'Neil, R., Welsh, M., Parke, R. D., Wang, S., & Strand, C. (1997). A longitudinal assessment of the academic correlates of early peer acceptance and rejection. *Journal of Clinical Child Psychology, 26,* 290–303.

52. Brackett, M. A., & Caruso, D. (2005). *The Emotionally Intelligent Teacher Workshop.* Ann Arbor, MI: Quest Education.

53. Teddlie, C., & Reynolds, D. (2000). *The international handbook of school effectiveness research.* London: Falmer.

54. Maurer, M., & Brackett, M. A. (2004). *Emotional literacy in the middle school: A six-step program to promote social, emotional, and academic learning.* Portchester, NY: National Professional Resources.

55. Brackett, M. A., Kremenitzer, J. P., Maurer, M., & Carpenter, M. (in press). *Emotional literacy in the elementary school.* Portchester, NY: National Professional Resources.

Richard E. Boyatzis

Developing Emotional Intelligence Competencies

James (a pseudonym for someone who prefers not to be identified) was confused about his future. It was odd because as Vice President of Information Technology at a mid-sized company he was doing quite well, or at least it appeared he was. Having grown up in a poor neighborhood in a Midwest city, he did much better than most of his friends – he lived. He went to college and was about to complete an EMBA. James loved his daughters and had a significant investment account ready to pay for their college. He was divorced, but on amiable terms with his ex-wife, and had a girl friend. He was devout in his faith, contributed his time eagerly to church projects, and was an advocate for Promise Keepers (a movement to encourage fathers to keep their promises to their families and their God). So what was wrong?

When James looked into his future, beyond a few months, it was a blank wall. It did not worry him, consciously. Like heartburn, he ignored his lack of an image for his future and hoped the discomfort would go away. His personal vision essay was devoted entirely to his family and his faith. As his coach, I asked him, "James, you didn't mention anything about work in your essay about your future. Do you have trust funds that you didn't mention?" He laughed, "No, I just thought I'd keep doing what I have been doing." Trying to invoke his passion about the future, I asked, "What would you love to do?"

After a long silence, he shrugged his shoulders. It seemed incongruous, a well-dressed, effective executive acting like a teenager who does not know what they want to have as a major in college. So I pushed, "If you won the Lottery, say $80 million dollars after tax, what would you do?" He told me that maybe he would drive a truck cross-country. This seemed more like an escape fantasy than a dream. A few minutes later, in response to a question as to what would make him feel truly happy that he was fulfilling his purpose in life, he said, "Teaching high school kids, in the inner city, that computers can be their instruments to freedom." Possibilities opened up for James. We talked about how he could teach workshops on Saturdays or Fridays at local high schools. He talked about setting up IT internships for high school students at local companies. It was as if a dam had opened and ideas flooded his consciousness. He leaned forward and was talking faster than I had heard him in months. The excitement was contagious – I could feel it. James had an epiphany. His image of his "work" in the future changed him from "been there, done that" to "Wow, I can't wait to get started." James now had a dream – a clear one he could work toward.

There are millions of Jameses working in organizations throughout the world. They want to be better professionals, managers, and leaders, but are puzzled as to how to reach that elusive goal. Or they believe they have done well and should be content – but not aspire to anything exciting in the future. With the best of intentions, they attend training programs, get MBAs, and hire consultants and coaches to help. And yet the degree of change is often small. They feel compelled to throw more resources into training, or slowly develop a belief that great professionals, managers, and leaders, are born, not made.

Emotional Intelligence Competencies

The most common mistake is to think that acquiring more knowledge will make you better. To be effective in most occupations, a person needs the ability to use their knowledge and to make things happen. These can be called competencies, which Boyatzis[1] defined as, "the underlying characteristics of a person that lead to or cause effective and outstanding performance." Whether direct empirical research is reviewed[1-6] or meta-analytic syntheses are used,[7,8] there are a set of competencies that have been shown to cause or predict outstanding professionals, managers, or leaders. Regardless of author or study, they tend to include abilities from three clusters: (1) cognitive or intellectual ability, such as systems thinking; (2) self-management or intrapersonal abilities, such as adaptability; and (3) relationship management or interpersonal abilities, such as networking. The latter two clusters make up what we call emotional intelligence competencies.[8-10]

The specific competencies (i.e., definitions) and behavioral indicators (i.e., alternate manifestations) emerge from a related stream of research that has emerged focusing on explaining and predicting effectiveness in various occupations, often with a primary emphasis on professionals, managers, and leaders.[1-4,7,11] In this "competency" approach, specific capabilities were identified and validated against effectiveness measures, or, often, inductively discovered and then articulated as competencies. So these competencies are inductively derived from effective or outstanding performance in various occupations in many countries. Of course, there are some threshold competencies (i.e., those needed to be an average performer), like functional or technical expertise, that are often acquired through prior experience. But we should not confuse experience (a threshold indicator) with a competency, which distinguishes average performers from top performers, and therefore effectiveness.

In addition to the distinctions noted above, a competency reflects an underlying construct, likely a more traditionally defined personality trait, ability, or motive. But it goes beyond that, to identify the related sets of patterns of behavior that are *alternate* manifestations of this underlying competency. This allows any person to vary the application of the competency depending on the needs and appropriateness to the specific setting.

For example, the competency called empathy can be observed by watching someone listen to others or asking questions about his or her feelings and thoughts. If one is demonstrating empathy, the person would be undertaking these acts with the intent of trying to understand another person. In contrast, someone could show these acts while cross-examining a witness in a criminal trial where the intent is to catch them in a lie – which is likely also to be the demonstration of another competency called influence.

Building upon and integrating a great deal of competency research, Goleman, Boyatzis, and McKee[9] presented a model of emotional intelligence with eighteen competencies arrayed in four clusters.[1,7,8] They are:

1. The Self-Awareness Cluster included Emotional Self-Awareness, Accurate Self-Assessment, and Self-confidence.
2. The Self-Management Cluster included Emotional Self-Control, Achievement, Initiative, Transparency, Adaptability, and Optimism.
3. The Social Awareness Cluster included Empathy, Service Orientation, and Organizational Awareness.
4. The Relationship Management Cluster included Inspirational Leadership, Influence, Conflict Management, Change Catalyst, Developing Others, Teamwork, and Collaboration.

Motivation and Drive

Beyond knowledge and competencies, the additional ingredient necessary for outstanding performance appears to be the desire to use one's talent. This seems driven by a person's values, philosophy, sense of calling or mission, unconscious motives, and traits. These three domains of capability (i.e., knowledge, competencies, and motivational drivers) help us to understand "what a person needs to do" (i.e., knowledge), "how a person needs to do it" (i.e., competencies), and "why a person will do it" (i.e., values, motives, and unconscious dispositions).

The assumption for too long has been that the competencies are inborn. This deterministic view has led to a focus on selection and placement rather than development. But these competencies, and in particular the ones called emotional intelligence, can be developed.

A growing body of research has helped us to discover a process that yields sustained behavioral change.[12,13] These improvements provide hope and evidence that people can develop the abilities, or competencies, that matter the most to outstanding performance, namely, the ones we call emotional intelligence (EI). Although the need to develop EI appears to be common sense, it is not common practice.

Can a Person Grow and Develop Their Talent?

Decades of research on the effects of psychotherapy,[14] self-help programs,[15] cognitive behavior therapy,[16] training programs,[17] and education[18] have shown that people can change their behavior, moods, and self-image. But most of the studies focused on a single characteristic, like maintenance of sobriety, reduction in a specific anxiety, or a set of characteristics often determined by the assessment instrument, such as the scales of the Minnesota Multiphasic Personality Inventory. There are few studies showing sustained improvements in the sets of desirable behavior that lead to outstanding performance.

The "honeymoon effect" of typical training programs might start with improvement immediately following the program, but within months it drops precipitously.[19] Only fifteen programs were found in a global search of the literature by the Consortium on Research on Emotional Intelligence in Organizations to improve emotional intelligence. Most of them showed an impact on job outcomes, such as number of new businesses started, or life outcomes, such as finding a job or satisfaction,[12] which are the ultimate purpose of development efforts. But even showing an impact on outcomes, while desired, may also blur *how* the change actually occurs. Furthermore, when a change has been noted, a question about the sustainability of the changes is raised because of the relatively short time periods studied.

The few published studies examining improvement of more than one of these competencies show an overall improvement of about 10% in EI abilities three to eighteen months following training.[20–24] More recent meta-analytic studies and utility analyses confirm that significant changes can and do occur, but not with the impact that the level of investment would lead us to expect, nor with many types of training.[17,25,26]

The results appear no better from standard MBA programs, where there is no attempt to enhance EI abilities. A major research project by the American Assembly of Collegiate Schools of Business found that receiving training from highly ranked business schools led to only a 2% increase in EI.[27] In fact, when students from four other high-ranking MBA programs were assessed on a range of tests and direct behavioral measures, they showed a gain of 4% in self-awareness and self-management abilities but a *decrease* of 3% in social awareness and relationship management.[28,29]

In contrast to these weak and inconsistent effects, recent findings suggest that some programs lead to long-term improvement in EI. A series of longitudinal studies underway at the Weatherhead School of Management of Case Western Reserve University have shown that people can change on EI and cognitive competencies that distinguish outstanding performers in management and professions. The improvement lasted for years, as shown with behavioral measures from different samples in Figure 2.1.

MBA students, averaging 27 years old at entry into the program, showed dramatic changes on videotaped and audiotaped behavioral samples and questionnaire measures of these competencies as a result of the competency-based, outcome-oriented MBA program implemented in 1990.[13] The studies were done with four cadres of full-time MBA students graduating in 1992, 1993, 1994, and 1995 and three cadres of part-time MBA students graduating in 1994, 1995, and 1996.

Perhaps the most impressive results came from Jane Wheeler,[30] who tracked down two cadres of the part-time MBAs two years *after* they had graduated. They showed improvements of 63% on the self-awareness and self-management competencies and 45% on the social awareness and relationship management competencies. This is in contrast to MBA graduates of the Weatherhead School of Management of the 1988 and 1989 traditional full-time and part-time program who showed improvement in substantially fewer of the competencies.

The positive effects of this program were not limited to MBAs. In a longitudinal study of four classes completing the Professional Fellows Program (i.e., an executive education program at the Weatherhead School of Management), Ballou, Bowers, Boyatzis, and Kolb[31] showed

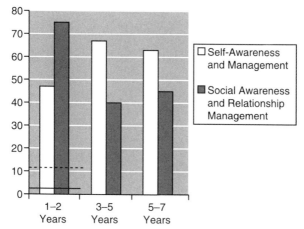

FIGURE 2.1 Percentage improvement of emotional intelligence from behavioral measurement of competencies of different groups of MBA graduates taking the Leadership Executive Assessment and Development course (for "n" and description of measures, see Reference 13; comparison references are listed in Reference 9). *Note:* (- - - -) Impact of company and government training programs 3–18 months after training on multiple emotional intelligence competencies; (———) impact of a variety of above average MBA programs.

that these 45–65-year-old professionals and executives improved on Self-Confidence, Leadership, Helping, Goal Setting, and Action skills. These were 67% of the EI competencies assessed in this study.

☐ Intentional Change

What the studies referred to above have shown is that adults learn what they want to learn. Other things, even if acquired temporarily (i.e., for a test), are soon forgotten.[32] Students, children, patients, clients, and subordinates may act as if they care about learning something, go through the motions, but they proceed to disregard it or forget it unless it is something that they want to learn.

In this way, it appears that most, if not all, sustainable behavioral change is intentional. *Intentional change is a desired change in an aspect of who you are (i.e., the Real) or who you want to be (i.e., the Ideal), or both.*

The process of intentional change is shown graphically in Figure 2.2.[9,33–35] This is an enhancement of the earlier models of Self-Directed Learning and Change developed by Kolb, Winter, and Berlew[36] and Kolb and Boyatzis.[37,38]

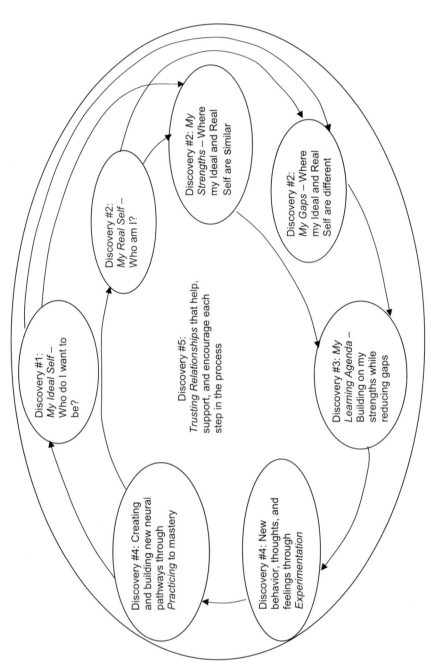

FIGURE 2.2 Boyatzis' Intentional Change Theory.

Change is a discontinuous process for most people. That is, it goes through "fits and starts" or surprises. In our previous example, James realized he had new dreams for the future, which unleashed a surge of energy and ideas for things he could do and how he could change his life. While these are often experienced as a conscious revelation or epiphany, we can call them discoveries. In complexity theory, these moments are called experiences of emergence. As a human, they often feel like discoveries or, even more spiritually, revelations. Whatever the experience, they are most often discontinuities in our experience.

Based on longitudinal studies of sustainable change, the description and explanation of the process in this chapter is organized around five points of discontinuity or emergence. We hypothesize that people are most likely to engage in sustainable or successful intentional change when they experience the five discoveries or discontinuities in sequence. The most adaptive people, those who sustain the changes, often go through the process of these five discoveries cyclically (i.e., repeatedly working through the cycle).

The Leadership Executive Assessment and Development Course

Our model of EI development focuses on a set of interventions that were integrated into a required MBA and executive courses implemented in 1990 at the Weatherhead School of Management. Years of experimentation and research into the various components have resulted in refinement of these components. For a detailed description of the course, see References 39 and 40.

One element that has always been a significant part of the experience is one-to-one coaching of each MBA or executive with faculty or advanced PhD students specially trained as coaches. The course design and how it aligns with Intentional Change Theory is described by Boyatzis[35] and is shown in Table 2.1.

MBAs have been criticized for decades for being too analytic and not ready to apply knowledge they have gained.[41-44] The Weatherhead School of Management sought to create a remedy for our graduates by developing a course in the MBA program that would help our students develop their competencies. This course was pilot tested in 1989 and then implemented as a required part of the full-time and part-time MBA in 1990 and the EMBA in 1998. It became a signature theme of the Weatherhead School of Management and was required in all degree programs (MBA, EMBA, PFP, EDM, TIME MS, MNO, MSPOD; a variation was required in the MSIS; and it was required for MACC for a number of years).

TABLE 2.1. Intentional Change Theory, the emotional intelligence development course, and course outputs

Intentional Change Theory	Course Elements	Course Outputs
Ideal Self	Values, operating philosophy Developing an image of your desired future: dreams, aspirations, fantasies, legacy, sense of purpose and passion Career aspirations and possibilities Family and personal health and spirituality vision Community vision Organizational vision	Personal Vision Essay
Real Self	Understanding emotional intelligence competencies and their impact on behavior, effectiveness, and leadership Videotaping exercises in small groups and/or presentations Collection of 360 views of others as to your frequency of showing different behaviors in the competencies (self, boss, subs, peers, customers/clients, friends, spouse/partner, friends, classmates)	Personal Balance Sheet and coaching session about your Personal Vision and Personal Balance Sheet
Learning Agenda	Learning Goals and Learning Plans Learning styles Planning styles	Learning Plan
Experimentation/ Practice	[Not included during course directly, although the preparation of the Learning Plan includes anticipating obstacles and stresses that might derail a person's efforts – relapse prevention in cognitive behavioral terms]	
Trusting Relationships	Peer coaching practice sessions	Relationship with a coach Relationship with a small group of peers for future and ongoing discussions

The overall objective of the Leadership Executive Assessment and Development (LEAD) course, or any of its variations, is: To learn a process for lifelong learning for yourself and others. To link to other chapters in this book, it could be said to focus on increasing one's mindfulness of their passion and purpose in life. The impact of the course is expected to be improvement on the competencies shown, in prior research, to predict outstanding performance or effectiveness in management, executive, leadership, entrepreneurial, and advanced professional jobs (like systems programmers, consultants, and analysts). Whether taught as a graduate degree course, a program for executives at the university, or provided within a specific company or organization, participants go through 20–45 hours of class or group work, supplemented with individual coaching.

There are four major outcomes from the course:

1. *A Personal Vision*: a clear statement as to what you want out of life (and work) and what kind of a person you wish to be/become.
2. *A Personal Balance Sheet*: an audit of your strengths and weaknesses, those that are deep and enduring and those that are close to the tipping point.
3. *A Learning Agenda and/or Plan* for how to move toward your Ideal Self (Personal Vision), using your strengths, possibly working on one or two weaknesses close to the tipping point – or a learning agenda to maintain the ideal state you currently are experiencing.
4. *Trusting*, if possible resonant relationships within which to assist intentional change in yourself and others.

The first third of the program is designed for each participant to create his/her own Personal Vision. This should reflect their full Ideal Self, which transcends their "best self" and strengths to arouse and incorporate their dreams, aspirations, and hope.[45] The program does not proceed until this benchmark is achieved in order to create the best physiological and emotional state within which a person may look at themselves and their desired future. The neural and hormonal state aroused opens the mind and maximizes the likelihood of learning.[34–46]

The second third of the program focuses on participants understanding the nature of emotional intelligence competencies, their link to effectiveness, and their physiological basis. Each person develops a personal balance sheet, through the use of a variety of assessment methods, including 360° assessments, videotapes and audiotapes of critical incidents from one's work and life, and simulations like those used in assessment centers. This outlines his/her strengths and distinctive strengths (reflecting an analogy to their current and long-term assets); weaknesses near the tipping point (those near the tipping point are shown or used frequently but not sufficiently to "tip" the person's performance into being outstanding or effective; they are the most likely to be changed sustainably; see References 6 and 11 for discussions of tipping points, of competencies, and their prediction of leadership performance) as an analogy to their current liabilities; and enduring dispositions, whether they be positively or negatively related to their performance at work or in life roles as an analogy to their net worth. The conversations with other participants in small groups using peer coaching are crucial at this stage of the process. The one-on-one discussions with a coach provided as part of the program staff are the most critical for a person's development of their Personal Vision, Personal Balance Sheet and Learning Agenda. The last third of the program focuses on developing a Learning Agenda in order to help participants to put their deepest desires into play.

Interaction with their peers becomes a vital aspect of every aspect of the program. This helps in the process of building resonant relationships and mutual caring. The modeling of compassion about helping people on their intentional change becomes an explicit topic as a method to take into their workplace, home, or community settings.[34,46]

The course is designed on the basis of two theories: (1) Boyatzis' Intentional Change Theory, as shown in Figure 2.2 and further described in the next section of this chapter; and (2) Kolb's[47] Experiential Learning Theory.

Course Impact

The major impact on sustained behavior change was discussed earlier in this chapter, as shown from the many longitudinal studies. These results earned the Weatherhead School of Management an award of one of the Fifteen Model Programs in the world in Developing Emotional Intelligence.[12] It is also thought to have contributed to the Number 1 Ranking of the Organizational Behavior Department at the Weatherhead School of Management in the *Financial Times* annual rankings of business schools in 2003, 2004, and 2005 (the first three years of rankings of Organizational Behaviour departments).[48] As an illustration of how students feel, course evaluations for MBA sections in the last four years are shown in Table 2.2.

There is a faculty member leading each section or the course, as well as teams of advanced professionals acting as personal coaches to the students or participants. The next section examines the design of the course and the process of intentional change.

☐ The First Discontinuity: Catching Your Dreams, Engaging Your Passion

The first discontinuity and potential starting point for the process of intentional change is the discovery of who you want to be. Our Ideal Self

TABLE 2.2. Last four years of course evaluations* for sections of the Leadership Executive
Assessment and Development course in the Weatherhead School of Management MBA
(number of students in the class in parentheses)

Year/Semester	Full-Time MBA	Part-Time MBA	EMBA
2004, Fall	4.66 (48)	4.72 (48)	–
	4.55 (45)	5.00 (35)	–
2004, Summer	4.73 (16)	4.79 (30)	–
2004, Spring	–	4.79 (18)	4.88 (43)
2003, Fall	4.37 (35)	4.54 (48)	–
	4.27 (34)	4,82 (43)	
2003, Summer	4.58 (29)	4.88 (17)	–
2003, Spring	–	4.81 (36)	4.58 (31)
		4.63 (22)	
		4.71 (17)	
2002, Fall	4.44 (39)	4.54 (47)	–
	3.72 (43)	3.31 (18)	
	4.46 (45)	4.63 (33)	
2002, Summer	4.40 (35)	4.77 (34)	–
2002, Spring	–	4.70 (46)	4.73 (32)
		4.47 (17)	
2002, Fall	4.19 (48)	4.79 (44)	–
	3.89 (53)	4.79 (30)	
	3.72 (50)		

* Evaluation ratings of the instructor on a scale of 1–5. School-wide average for MBA-required
courses is 4.0.

is an image of the person we want to be.[45] It emerges from our ego ideal,
dreams, and aspirations. The last twenty years has revealed literature
supporting the power of positive imaging or visioning in sports
psychology, meditation and biofeedback research, and other psycho-
physiological research. It is believed that the potency of focusing one's
thoughts on the desired end state is driven by the emotional components
of the brain.[49]

This research indicates that we can access and engage deep emotional
commitment if we engage our passions and conceptually integrate our
dreams in our Ideal Self image. It is an anomaly that we know the importance of the Ideal Self, and yet often, when engaged in a change or learning
process, we skip over the clear formulation or articulation of our Ideal Self
image. If a parent, spouse, boss, or teacher tells us something that should
be different, they are telling us about the person *they* want us to be. As
adults, we often allow ourselves to be anesthetized to our dreams and lose
sight of our deeply felt Ideal Self.

Personal Vision: My Ideal Self

Although the specifics of a person's vision vary tremendously, here are several excerpts from the concluding portion of the Personal Vision essay.

Frank: "To begin, my greatest aspiration is to keep a happy, healthy family together for a very long time. This means continued strengthening of my marriage, and being surrounded by my children and future grandchildren. . . . Yes my first life aspiration is not one of money at all, but happiness with the people closest to me. However, as I stated earlier, happiness is not enough. I must also find financial freedom and acquire the resources to make everyone's life better. . . .

Social security begins at age 65, with full benefits paid at 68. My current company's retirement benefits begin at 60 with full benefits at 65. College for kids begins in 5 years, ending 13 years later. At 41 years old this means I need to plan for 20 to 30 more years of career. . . .

In all due respect for my current company who pays for this education, I begin with the intent of life long service to this company. . . . But now, . . . I am disappointed that the hard work and time away from my family has only resulted in this [District manager].

The second phase of my career began with enrollment in this program. . . . Instead, I decided to live this half of my life with different expectations. Rather than grateful for my current situation, I needed to expect more. Therefore, I applied for tuition reimbursement for this program.

. . . Enrolling here gave me purpose and focus again. Pressure has always brought out the best in me, and I've been able to achieve straight A's while our sales district rose from 18th to 3rd in the nation. . . .

Remaining at my company probably means moving to a product division that offers P & L responsibility. . . . Moving to a product division means learning process and procedures used in the daily chug of the business. . . . I see no value in learning stuff that those before me have already perfected. While this is referred to as "rounding out" one's experience, it seems like no job for the inspired. My vision of success is employing a great plant manager, not being one, hiring the top marketer, not studying under one. . . .

In planning future moves, I believe in looking out 10 years to the perfect state. To me, this will be everything described in section two of this paper. So if I am to run a company, will it be my current employer? . . .

One position really excites me, strategic development. . . . A position such as this could get me closer to the end goal while offering travel and interface with new people. . . . I find true satisfaction in situations where my knowledge is needed and respected by others. Therefore, a position with a smaller company may be in order. . . . I could see a position as Vice President of Sales or even President of a company whose top priority is growth and customer relations. . . .

A Senior VP or CEO of a smaller organization struggling for growth [is attractive] – a private firm looking for professional management which includes a succession plan offering ownership. . . .

How about starting that candy company? [a dream job mentioned in an exercise] I could certainly start small, mixing batches of my grandma's hard tack in the basement while working to grow into the first factory. For this to become a real option, I must free time. Concentrate on freeing time from current demands to invest in my future. In a few short months I will free a lot of time.

With this vision of several possible career paths, Frank had to work out a Learning Plan that helped him to first choose the best path while moving toward his family vision. Competency development, if it is to occur, has to be tied to a compelling vision. It has to serve a higher purpose. To sustain a habit change, the competency development must be more than an instrumental need, like the need to learn calculus if you are to pass a graduate finance course.

Barbara: "Looking over my history and what drives me to action, I am especially impassioned by the lack of customer service in the U.S. business world today and I have a strong passion for creating something new. . . . Customer service would have to be . . . given a fresh outlook. I feel that stories can make this happen . . . by becoming a funnel for these stories, I can help to spread the word on . . . customer service. I would also use this information as training aids and to develop a measurement tool for a business to track their progress. . . .

My background has been heavily in engineering and marketing. Personally, I feel that I have been held back by my own internal lack of self-confidence. My own "self-talk" did not allow me to see that I am even "worthy" of accomplishing things. Even writing this now is difficult because I have never thought about the possibility of making an impact and what it would look like.

Doors to new opportunities have been opened to me in my dreaming of what could be and how I want to participate in making it happen. My coach has helped me to see the possibilities. I truly believe that women today need an inspirational coach, role model, or confidante to provide encouragement. . . . I see myself working with young women/teens in the future to help them see their own potential and all of the possibilities – to expand their horizons.

I envision my path toward these goals to first include a job change to a customer-centric environment. . . . I would also want to participate directly in the training and strategy development. . . . I would use specific cases as examples for future training or possibly a book. Day-to-day life experiences would bring me a smorgasbord of examples. . . .

With this background, I envision breaking out on my own to create a platform for Customer Service. It would consist of a training tool and benchmark measures for companies to learn from. Implementation procedures and guides would be created. A website would be established for feedback and input by market segment to provide additional data or insights. . . .

With success in this avenue and the added personal flexibility, I would pursue setting up my own company as a spring-board for an entrepreneurial team. It would provide consulting or practical procedures/training for applying true customer service ethics throughout the business culture of a company. This step then provides additional contacts and networks that would be used to supplement the goal to work with or establish a teenage women's entrepreneurial group.

A close tie with the educational system would be critical. . . . I would need a solid educational partner with background in this area, possibly through a local university. In addition, I would also need an experienced person in the not-for-profit arena and a network of successful female entrepreneurs. I am currently noting the network capabilities of Women Millionaires.com as a starting point for format of website and for contacts.

My desired lifestyle would be to have the freedom to impact the young people the way I want to, the time to also be able to enjoy travel and to play golf, and to share my remaining years with Charles while still healthy. . . .

I want to be the kind of person that is remembered for making the world at least a slightly better place. . . . To be remembered for improving customer service in the business world and to have impacted how teens see entering the business world would be a true accomplishment for me.

This process has given me a new insight into the direction of my life. I feel more in control of my life rather than having to let life just simply happen to me. Going forward, I will continue to make steps toward this dream and make decisions according to what the outcome should look like. . . .

Barbara needed to develop her self-confidence to enable progress toward her personal and career vision. It was an ability that was close to, but still below, the tipping point. Development of self-confidence was feasible and sustainable because, again, it served a deep-felt purpose or passion. As she said, the process of developing her Personal Vision *began* the change process. Developing a clearer, or emerging view of the Ideal Self and Personal Vision is the first major step. Now comes the assessment of one's strengths to help people achieve their vision and weaknesses that might act as barriers.

☐ The Second Discontinuity: Am I a Boiling Frog?

The awareness of the current self, the person that others see and with whom they interact, is elusive. Our mind protects us from potentially noxious or threatening input to our conscious realization about ourselves. These are ego-defense mechanisms. They also conspire to delude us into an image of who we are that feeds on itself, becomes self-perpetuating, and eventually may become dysfunctional.[50]

The greatest challenge to an accurate current self-image (i.e., seeing yourself as others see you and consistent with other internal states, beliefs, emotions, and so forth) is the boiling frog syndrome. It is said that dropping a frog into a pot of boiling water will result in it immediately jumping out. But place a frog in a pot of cool water, and gradually raise the temperature to boiling, and the frog will remain in the water until it is cooked.

Several factors contribute to us becoming boiling frogs. First, people around you may not let you see a change. They may not give you feedback or information about how they see it. Also, they may be victims of the boiling frog syndrome themselves, as they adjust their perception on a daily basis. Second, enablers, those forgiving the change, frightened of it, or who do not care, may allow it to pass unnoticed.

For people to truly consider changing a part of himself or herself, they must have a sense of what they value and want to keep. The areas in which your Real Self and Ideal Self are consistent or congruent can be considered strengths. Likewise, to consider what you want to preserve about yourself involves admitting aspects of yourself that you wish to change or adapt in some manner. Areas where your Real Self and Ideal Self are not consistent can be considered gaps, or weaknesses.

All too often, people explore growth or development by focusing on the "gaps" or deficiencies. Organizational training programs and managers conducting annual reviews often make the same mistake. There is an assumption that we can "leave well enough alone" and get to the areas that need work. This arouses defense and tension, which in turn set off a neural circuit and hormones that decrease a person's ability to learn and stay focused.[34] It is no wonder that many of these procedures intended to help a person develop result in the individual feeling battered, beleaguered, and bruised, not helped, encouraged, motivated, or guided.

☐ The Third Discontinuity: Mindfulness through a Learning Agenda

The third discontinuity in intentional change is development of an agenda and focusing on the desired future. While performance at work or happiness in life may be the eventual consequence of these efforts, a learning agenda focuses on the concrete actions needed for development. A learning orientation arouses a positive belief in one's capability and the hope of improvement. This results in people setting personal standards of performance, rather than "normative" standards that merely mimic what others have done.[51] Meanwhile, a performance orientation evokes anxiety and doubts about whether or not we can change.[52]

As part of one of the longitudinal studies at the Weatherhead School of Management, Leonard[53] showed that MBAs who set goals desiring to change on certain competencies changed significantly on those competencies as compared to MBAs who did not set goals. Previous goal-setting literature had shown how goals affected certain changes on specific competencies,[54] but had not established evidence of behavioral change on a comprehensive set of competencies that constitute EI.

A major threat to effective goal setting and planning is that people are already busy and cannot add anything else to their lives. In such cases, successful change only occurs if people can determine what to say "no" to and stop – to make room for new activities.

Another potential threat to the development of a plan is one that calls for a person to engage in activities different than their preferred learning style or learning flexibility.[39,47] When this occurs, a person becomes demotivated and often stops the activities, or becomes impatient and decides that the goals are not worth the effort. Unintentionally, this is one of many ways people may sabotage their change effort before it gets started. In other words, if your personal learning style preference is concrete experience, then attending a lecture or academic course will turn you off to learning, not motivate it.[47] For a person with such a learning style preference, participating in action learning or projects is exciting and maintains the motivation needed to sustain work on change.

Examples of Learning Plans

To be effective, a person has to turn the desire and hope of the Personal Vision into a workable plan of action. The Learning Plan is that vehicle. But it is only the overview. It is the power of the Ideal Self and vision that drives the person to do these actions. The reminders and support from key people keep them going on the plan. Here are examples of Learning Plan outlines from two people. The EI competencies to be developed are listed in bold italics below.

Example Learning Plan 1

Arthur wanted to improve his Empathy and Developing Others competencies. He already used them well and frequently with subordinates, but not with peers or social networks. He also felt that he needed to increase his Communications competency by consistently giving inspirational presentations. Let us look at how he intended to do this.

1. Think of all stakeholders as subordinates (Engage Them).
   a. Motivate people to do work for me instead of doing the work myself.
      - Become a mentor to a non-subordinate employee *(Develop others)* (1–3 months and ongoing).
      - Develop a cross-functional team and lead them through a project without "doing any of the work" (1–3 months and ongoing).
      - Delegate more operational responsibility to subordinates (immediately and ongoing).
   b. Show concern for the others' life *(Develop others)*.
      - Take the time to hear others out.
      - Concentrate on listening and caring about their position.
      - Do not cut them off and jump to my own conclusions early.
   c. Develop presentation skills *(Communications)*.
      - Volunteer to present in more "unfamiliar" business settings (immediately and ongoing).
      - Join an organization like Toastmasters to improve presentation skills (3 months).
      - Become active in the business operations of my wife's church which will require frequent presentations to a diverse group (immediate and ongoing).
   d. Improve *Empathy*.
      - Understand other person's perspective of a problem (immediate and ongoing).
      - Listen to my wife without attempting to solve her problem (ongoing).
2. Family/Work balance lifestyle.
   a. Be home by 7:00 pm to eat dinner as a family (immediately and ongoing).
   b. Take a two-week family vacation every year (starting in June and ongoing).
   c. Make third Saturday of every month "date night" with my wife (immediately and ongoing).
   d. Commit to my family the same way I commit to my job (immediately and ongoing).
3. Find a small manufacturing business to buy and build or start and build (2–4 years).
   a. Identify and acquire capital (6–12 months).
      - Investigate Small Business Administration financing options.
      - Investigate traditional bank financing options.
      - Investigate Family/Friends investing options.
      - Investigate business network financing options.

b. Identify potential acquisition targets based on capital available (6–18 months).
- Establish relationship with business broker.
- Identify area(s) of interest for business opportunities (East and Southeast).
- Develop a list of potential acquisition candidates.
- Rank listing based on attractiveness of industry, price, and location.

c. Negotiate and finalize acquisition (3–6 months).

Example Learning Plan 2

Marjorie had a tremendous amount of talent, but lately she found herself drifting. She was doing professional or executive jobs but not loving them. As a result, she did not bring all of her talent to work everyday. She knew that her passion was in landscape development. She knew her strengths were in networking, marketing, and selling. But she wanted to find a way to fit it all together in a more meaningful life.

1. Find a job or create a career that provides an opportunity to use my skills and talents in land use management and/or creative communications, and provides the freedom to make decisions and choices and the financial security to live a comfortable life.
   a. Sub-goal: Meet or interview with people in organizations that meet the above criteria. People I have talked with recently:
      - Sam and Frank who gave me suggestions that included offering business development skills to organizations like the City Garden, land and real estate developers, and others.
      - ABC gave me information about the area's non-profit organizations and people to contact.
      - Fred offers me opportunities to write copy and develop business but he drags his feet on commitment to new business.
      - Bob has potential opportunities in the future.
      - Various opportunities for public relations work but I do not think it will lead me closer to my ideal life because I am not good at selling something unless I believe in it.
   b. Sub-goal: Submit application materials to various announced positions.
      - Director and other admin jobs at the City Garden and other land use agencies.
      - Consulting positions with environmental consulting firms.
   c. Sub-goal: Explore creating my own company doing business development.

- Write and propose business development plan to Bill, Director at the City Garden.
- Propose same to land development companies.
2. Meet someone with whom I can be intimate.
   a. Sub-goal: Get out more where I can meet people my age, with my interests, who are single.
   b. Sub-goal: Do the things I love and therefore meet other people who like those things – golf, travel, hiking, etc.
3. Exercise and eat better.
   a. Sub-goal: Finish the EMBA! Saturday mornings will be mine again and I can take care of life.
   b. Sub-goal: Make a schedule that allows me to exercise early in the day when I have the energy.
   c. Sub-goal: Resume some of the activities I love, like hiking, photography, and sports.
4. Organize home and work so I can better accomplish goals.
   a. Sub-goal: Take a day to organize the basement.
   b. Sub-goal: Hire help to do "fix-it" jobs on the house, trim the tree that lost limbs in the winter storm, and mow and edge the lawn.
   c. Sub-goal: Get filing under control.

Marjorie needed a new focus on life. First, she felt she had to, literally, get "her house in order," and prepare herself for the two major goals: (1) a new, focused career; and (2) find a loving relationship. In her case, competency development was really competency application. She had stopped using the EI abilities she already had. She needed to think of herself as a business development project to re-engage her talent.

☐ The Fourth Discontinuity: Metamorphosis

The fourth discontinuity involves practicing desired changes. This is the part of the process where the change occurs. We can envision a change, but only when we practice it and receive feedback from internally and our environment does the change begin to form as a new habit. Continued practice in various settings increases the likelihood that the new behavior becomes a habit. Life becomes our learning laboratory. Acting on the plan and toward the goals involves numerous activities. These are often made in the context of experimenting with new behavior or rediscovering an ability used well in the past but not in the person's current repertoire or habits. Typically following a period of experimentation, the person practices the new behaviors in actual settings within which they wish to use them, such as at work or at home. During this part of the process, intentional change begins to look like a "continuous improvement" process.

To develop or learn new behavior, the person must find ways to learn more from current or ongoing experiences. That is, the experimentation and practice do not always require attending "courses" or a new activity. It may involve mindfulness – trying something different in a current setting, reflecting on what occurs, and experimenting further in this setting. Sometimes, this part of the process requires finding and using opportunities to learn and change. People may not even think they have changed until they have tried new behavior in a work or "real world" setting.

Dreyfus[55] studied managers of scientists and engineers who were considered superior performers. Once she documented that they used considerably more of certain abilities than their less effective counterparts, she pursued how they developed some of those abilities. One of the distinguishing abilities was Group Management, also called Team Building. She found that many of these middle-aged managers had first experimented with team building skills in high school and college, in sports, clubs, and living groups. Later, when they became "bench scientists and engineers" working on problems in relative isolation, they still pursued the use and practice of this ability in activities outside of work. They practiced team building and group management in social and community organizations, such as 4-H Clubs, and professional associations in planning conferences and such.

The experimentation and practice are most effective when they occur in conditions in which the person feels safe.[38] This sense of psychological safety creates an atmosphere in which the person can try new behavior, perceptions, and thoughts with relatively less risk of shame, embarrassment, or serious consequences of failure. The challenge is to practice to the point of mastery, not merely the point of comfort.

☐ The Fifth Discontinuity: Relationships that Enable Us to Learn

Our relationships are an essential part of our environment. The most crucial relationships are often a part of groups that have particular importance to us. These relationships and groups give us a sense of identity, guide us as to what is appropriate and "good" behavior, and provide feedback on our behavior. In sociology, they are called reference groups. These relationships create a "context" within which we interpret our progress on desired changes, the utility of new learning, and even contribute significant input to formulation of the Ideal.[56]

In this sense, our relationships are mediators, moderators, interpreters, sources of feedback, sources of support, and permission to change and learn. They may also be the most important source of protection from returning to our earlier forms of ineffective behavior. Wheeler[30] analyzed the extent to which the MBA graduates worked on their goals in multiple "life spheres" (i.e., work, family, recreational groups, etc.). In a two-year follow-up study of two of the graduating classes of part-time MBA students, she found that those who worked on their goals and plans in multiple sets of relationships improved the most compared to those who worked on their goals in only one setting (e.g., at work).

In the studies of the impact of the year-long executive development program, Ballou et. al.[31] found that the program increased self-confidence amongst doctors, lawyers, professors, engineers, and other professionals. This finding was interesting because these professionals appeared, on the surface, to already have high self-confidence. How could any program increase it? The best explanation came from follow-up questions to the graduates of the program. The increase in self-confidence seemed to occur because the graduates had greater trust in their ability to change. Their existing reference groups (i.e., family, groups at work, professional groups, community groups) all had an investment in them staying the same, whereas the person wanted to change. The Professional Fellows Program allowed them to develop a new reference group that created more "psychological space" for change.

Our relationships are critical to our sense of who we are and who we want to be. We develop or elaborate our Ideal Self from these contexts. We label and interpret our Real Self from these contexts. We interpret and value strengths (i.e., aspects considered our core that we wish to preserve) and gaps (i.e., aspects considered weaknesses or things we wish to change) from these contexts.

☐ Concluding Thought

Just as James found, or refound, his passion in his work, Frank, Barbara, Arthur, and Marjorie had to develop a new Personal Vision before seriously engaging in change. Adults can develop leadership and emotional intelligence but they have to deeply want the change to occur, otherwise they cannot sustain the effort or overcome lethargy and the obstacles. Behavioral change is feasible only in the context of a positive, personal vision and caring relationships. Through intentional change theory and process, coaches can help someone make their dreams come alive. Through this process and help, we have the opportunity to truly make a difference. Whether applied in universities or companies, government agencies or not-for-profits, this process can help us coach each other to create the social environments we want and find so conducive to making a difference.

☐ References

1. Boyatzis, R. E. (1982). *The competent manager: A model for effective performance.* New York: John Wiley & Sons.
2. Kotter, J. P. (1982). *The general managers.* New York: Free Press.
3. Thornton, G. C. III, & Byham, W. C. (1982). *Assessment centers and managerial performance.* New York: Academic Press.
4. Luthans, F., Hodgetts, R. M., & Rosenkrantz, S. A. (1988). *Real managers.* Cambridge, MA: Ballinger Press.
5. Howard, A., & Bray, D. (1988). *Managerial lives in transition: Advancing age and changing times.* New York: Guilford Press.
6. Boyatzis, R. E. (2006). Using tipping points of emotional intelligence and cognitive competencies to predict financial performance of leaders. *Psicothemia, 17,* 124–131.
7. Spencer, L. M. Jr., & Spencer, S. M. (1993). *Competence at work: Models for superior performance.* New York: John Wiley & Sons.
8. Goleman, D. (1998). *Working with emotional intelligence.* New York: Bantam Books.
9. Goleman, D., Boyatzis, R. E., & McKee, A. (2002). *Primal leadership: Realizing the power of emotional intelligence.* Boston: Harvard Business School Press.
10. Boyatzis, R. E., & Sala, F. (2004). Assessing emotional intelligence competencies. In G. Geher (Ed.), *The measurement of emotional intelligence* (pp. 147–180). Hauppauge, NY: Nova Science Publishers.
11. McClelland, D. C. (1973). Testing for competence rather than intelligence. *American Psychologist, 28,* 1–14.
12. Cherniss, C., & Adler, M. (2000). *Promoting emotional intelligence in organizations: Make training in emotional intelligence effective.* Washington, DC: American Society of Training and Development.
13. Boyatzis, R. E., Stubbs, E. C., & Taylor, S. N. (2002). Learning cognitive and emotional intelligence competencies through graduate management education. *Academy of Management Journal on Learning and Education, 1,* 150–162.
14. Hubble, M. A., Duncan, B. L., & Miller, S. D. (1999). *The heart and soul of change: What works in therapy.* Washington, DC: American Psychological Association.
15. Kanfer, F. H., & Goldstein, A. P. (1991). *Helping people change: A textbook of methods* (4th ed.). Boston: Allyn and Bacon.
16. Barlow, D. H. (1988). *Anxiety and disorders: The nature and treatment of anxiety and panic.* New York: The Guilford Press.
17. Morrow, C. C., Jarrett, M. Q., & Rupinski, M. T. (1997). An investigation of the effect and economic utility of corporate-wide training. *Personnel Psychology, 50,* 91–119.
18. Pascarella, E. T., & Terenzini, P. T. (1991). *How college affects students: Findings and insights from twenty years of research.* San Francisco: Jossey-Bass.
19. Campbell, J. P., Dunnette, M. D., Lawler, E. E. III, & Weick, K. E. (1970). *Managerial behavior, performance, and effectiveness.* New York: McGraw-Hill.
20. Noe, R. A., & Schmitt, N. (1986). The influence of trainee attitudes on training effectiveness: Test of a model. *Personnel Psychology, 39,* 497–523.

21. Hand, H. H., Richards, M. D., & Slocum, J. W. Jr. (1973). Organizational climate and the effectiveness of a human relations training program. *Academy of Management Journal, 16,* 185–246.
22. Wexley, K. N., & Memeroff, W. F. (1975). Effectiveness of positive reinforcement and goal setting as methods of management development. *Journal of Applied Psychology, 60,* 446–450.
23. Latham, G. P., & Saari, L. M. (1979). Application of Social-learning Theory to training supervisors through behavioral modeling. *Journal of Applied Psychology, 64,* 239–246.
24. Young, D. P., & Dixon, N. M. (1996). *Helping leaders take effective action: A program evaluation.* Greensboro, NC: Center for Creative Leadership.
25. Baldwin, T., & Ford, J. K. (1988). Transfer of training: A review and directions for future research. *Personnel Psychology, 41,* 63–105.
26. Burke, M. J., & Day, R. R. (1986). A cumulative study of the effectiveness of managerial training. *Journal of Applied Psychology, 71,* 232–245.
27. Development Dimensions International (DDI) (1985). *Final report: Phase III.* Report to the American Assembly of Collegiate Schools of Business, St. Louis, MO.
28. Boyatzis, R. E., & Sokol, M. (1982). *A pilot project to assess the feasibility of assessing skills and personal characteristics of students in collegiate business programs.* Report to the American Assembly of Collegiate Schools of Business, St. Louis, MO.
29. Boyatzis, R. E., Renio-McKee, A., & Thompson, L. (1995). Past accomplishments: Establishing the impact and baseline of earlier programs. In R. E. Boyatzis, S. S. Cowen, & D. A. Kolb (Eds.), *Innovation in professional education: Steps on a journey from teaching to learning.* San Francisco: Jossey-Bass.
30. Wheeler, J. V. (1999). The impact of social environments on self-directed change and learning. Unpublished Doctoral Dissertation, Case Western Reserve University.
31. Ballou, R., Bowers, D., Boyatzis, R. E., & Kolb, D. A. (1999). Fellowship in lifelong learning: An executive development program for advanced professionals. *Journal of Management Education, 23,* 338–354.
32. Specht, L., & Sandlin, P. (1991). The differential effects of experiential learning activities and traditional lecture classes in accounting. *Simulations and Gaming, 22,* 196–210.
33. Boyatzis, R. E. (2001) How and why individuals are able to develop emotional intelligence. In C. Cherniss and D. Goleman (Eds.), *The emotionally intelligent workplace: How to select for, measure, and improve emotional intelligence in individuals, groups, and organizations* (pp. 234–253). San Francisco: Jossey-Bass.
34. Boyatzis, R., & McKee, A. (2005). *Resonant leadership: Renewing yourself and connecting with others through mindfulness, hope and compassion.* Boston: Harvard Business School Press.
35. Boyatzis, R. E. (2006). Intentional change theory from a complexity perspective. *Journal of Management Development, 25,* 607–623.
36. Kolb, D. A., Winter, S. K., & Berlew, D. E. (1968). Self-directed change: Two studies. *Journal of Applied Behavioral Science, 6,* 453–471.
37. Kolb, D. A., & Boyatzis, R. E. (1970). On the dynamics of the helping relationship. *Journal of Applied Behavioral Science, 6,* 267–289.
38. Kolb, D. A., & Boyatzis, R. E. (1970). Goal-setting and self-directed behavior change. *Human Relations, 23,* 439–457.
39. Boyatzis, R. E. (1994). Stimulating self-directed change: A required MBA course called Managerial Assessment and Development. *Journal of Management Education, 18,* 304–323.
40. Boyatzis, R. E. (1995). Cornerstones of change: Building a path for self-directed learning. In R. E. Boyatzis, S. C. Cowen, & D. A. Kolb (Eds.), *Innovation in professional education: Steps on a journey from teaching to learning* (pp. 50–94). San Francisco: Jossey-Bass.

41. Porter, L., & McKibbin, L. (1988). *Management education and development: Drift or thrust into the 21st century?* New York: McGraw-Hill.

42. Pfeffer, J., & Fong, C. T. (2002). The end of business schools? Less success than meets the eye. *Academy of Management Learning and Education, 1,* 78–95.

43. Mintzberg, H. (2004). *Managers not MBAs: A hard look at the soft practice of managing and management development.* New York: Prentice Hall.

44. Bennis, W., & O'Toole, J. (2005). How business schools lost their way. *Harvard Business Review,* May.

45. Boyatzis, R. E., & Akrivou-Naperksy, K. (2006). The ideal self as a driver of change. *Journal of Management Development, 25,* 624–642.

46. Boyatzis, R. E., Smith, M., & Blaize, N. (2006). Developing sustainable leaders through coaching and compassion. *Academy of Management Journal on Learning and Education, 5,* 8–24.

47. Kolb, D. A. (1984). *Experiential learning: Experience as the source of learning and development.* Englewood Cliffs, NJ: Prentice Hall.

48. Bradshaw, D. (2003, 2004, 2005). Ranking MBA programs and specialty areas. *Financial Times.*

49. Goleman, D. (1995). *Emotional intelligence.* New York: Bantam Books.

50. Goleman, D. (1985). *Vital lies, simple truths: The psychology of self-deception.* New York: Simon and Schuster.

51. Beaubien, J. M., & Payne, S. C. (1999). Individual goal orientation as a predictor of job and academic performance: A meta-analytic review and integration. Paper presented at the meeting of the Society for Industrial and Organizational Psychology, Atlanta, GA, April 1999.

52. Chen, G., Gully, S. M., Whiteman, J. A., & Kilcullen, R. N. (2000). Examination of relationships among trait-like individual differences, state-like individual differences, and learning performance. *Journal of Applied Psychology, 85,* 835–847.

53. Leonard, D. (1996). *The impact of learning goals on self-directed change in management development and education.* Doctoral Dissertation, Case Western Reserve University.

54. Locke, E. A., & Latham, G. P. (1990). *A theory of goal setting and task performance.* Englewood Cliffs, NJ: Prentice Hall.

55. Dreyfus, C. (1990). *The characteristics of high performing managers of scientists and engineers.* Unpublished Doctoral Dissertation, Case Western Reserve University.

56. Kram, K. E. (1996) A relational approach to careers. In D. T. Hall (Ed.), *The career is dead: Long live the career* (pp. 132–157). San Francisco: Jossey-Bass Publishers.

Susan A. Kornacki
David R. Caruso

CHAPTER 3

A Theory-Based, Practical Approach to Emotional Intelligence Training: Ten Ways to Increase Emotional Skills

Imagine you have traveled to a place that was inhabited by Sneetches, the whimsical characters invented by Theodor Geisel, otherwise known as "Dr. Seuss." When you arrive in the land of Sneetches, you quickly discover that there are two different types of creatures: those with "stars upon thars" and those with no stars upon their bellies. In our version of the Seuss tale, the no-star Sneetches are those that *only* value facts and tangible forms of data in their decision making and shun the use of emotion in making decisions. The star-bellied Sneetches *only* value emotion in their decision making and have little regard for numbers, analysis and rationality.

If you were to become a Sneetch, which kind would you be? Which sort of Sneetch is the smarter, more intelligent Sneetch? Emotion Sneetches or non-emotion Sneetches? In fact, it is rather difficult to imagine how either of these two types of creatures would perform in our world, or in theirs, because our daily decision making combines both logic and emotion. Some of us may lean more toward logic and data, and may be construed as being "cold" or "overly rational." And others lean toward both expressing and valuing emotions, and may be construed as being "overly emotional."

Discussions about emotions and especially about emotional intelligence (EI) often pit extremes against one another – an all-emotion Sneetch versus a pure-logic Sneetch. Yet, EI is not about being illogical or overly emotional, it is about the intelligent use of emotions and utilizing the information contained in emotions to make effective decisions. A person who you may consider to be an emotional person, conveying sadness, anger, and happiness on a regular basis, does not necessarily equate to an emotionally intelligent person. Conversely, a person who may not overtly express those emotions may be emotionally intelligent.

Emotions can evoke a behavioral response, even when one is unaware of the emotion. Our understanding and expression of emotions can move from the subconscious to a level of consciousness where we ultimately realize we have the skills to understand and manage emotions.

Emotions may be largely unconscious and may drive behavior, unaided by much logic or reasoning. Unfortunately, such emotional behavior can be impulsive and inconsistent with what people actually value. For example, many individuals push others away even though they are in need of emotional support from other people. Given the apparent downsides of emotion, one may choose to rely entirely on reason and ignore emotions. Unfortunately, research shows that disregarding emotions can lead to bad decision making.[1,2]

If you do not recall how Seuss' story concludes, the star-bellied Sneetches and no-star Sneetches discover that neither holds the key to a happy life. Simply, they need each other. Our chapter will hopefully bring you to the same conclusion: effective decision making and action require both rationality and emotion.

☐ Chapter Goals

Our main goal for writing this chapter is to increase the readers' EI knowledge and skills in a fairly easy to understand, logical, and engaging format. We will do this by incorporating activities throughout the chapter, outlining learning outcomes, and understanding the different abilities required to use emotions intelligently. The reader will have the opportunity to examine case studies and practice EI developmental exercises. While this chapter is designed for use in individual development, the skilled facilitator can readily adapt the exercises for use in group settings.

First we must lay some ground work regarding the definition of the ability model of EI, learn what good and not so good EI behavior looks like, and discuss the importance of what it takes to acquire new information to ultimately enhance our behavior to use emotions intelligently. It is our desire that those people who read this chapter are left with a framework regarding the ability model of EI, are motivated to learn these skills, and can immediately find application of this knowledge from the information and activities presented in this chapter.

☐ Ability-Based Emotional Intelligence Development

Laying the Groundwork

Emotional intelligence is defined as "the ability to perceive emotions, to access and generate emotions so as to assist thought, to understand emotions and emotional knowledge, and to reflectively regulate emotions so as to promote emotional and intellectual growth."[3]

The modern field of EI saw its first scientific publication in 1990 and is still relatively new. Its developers, Mayer and Salovey, and through later collaboration with Caruso, have enhanced the ability model and created a process model of EI which they call an "emotional blueprint."[4] The four abilities proposed by Mayer and Salovey are (1) the ability to accurately perceive emotions and to express emotions, (2) the ability to generate emotions and use them to help you solve problems, (3) the ability to understand the causes of emotions and their progressions and combinations, and (4) the ability to manage emotions so as to have them enhance decision making. In turn, the Emotional Blueprint turns this hierarchical model into a process model where emotions are first identified or perceived, the emotions are used to influence attention and thinking, we attempt to understand emotional causes and transitions, and we manage the emotions so as to act intelligently with, and on, the data in these emotions.

Emotional intelligence is both *intrapersonal* and *interpersonal*. Intrapersonal is EI within ourselves: how we take in and process emotional information affecting our individual thoughts and behaviors. Interpersonal is EI that occurs when two or more people interact. There is also an influencing aspect of interpersonal EI, which we will discuss later in the chapter.

We recognize that the ability model of EI at times may seem like logical, common sense. However, there is beauty in its simplicity. Using the framework that emotions contain highly valuable information, those people who are able to understand how to harness that information achieve better relational outcomes than those who are not able to use EI. We discuss these areas because in order for someone to want to learn how to use a new skill, it had better be something that can help immediately enhance your life.

Learning Skills and Personal Payoffs

So what is the payoff for learning how to use emotions intelligently? As you are beginning to explore EI and determine if this is something that is worthy of your time and energy and perhaps the time and energy of others, it is important to understand what we know about EI. Why is this important? It is important because we have good recent data which suggest that EI is related to performance in a wide variety of areas that impact you both now and in years to come. Team functioning, leadership effectiveness, and improved communication have all been found to be related to EI.[5–7] Unlike other skills that you may or may not use often, EI is something that you will use on a daily basis.

Lastly, a large part of laying groundwork is a focus on you, the learner. We have included a self-check activity, which is designed to have you examine how you best learn a new skill. The old adage comes into play, "you can lead a horse to water, but you can't make it drink." Finding out what makes that individual thirsty (motivated) enough to drink the water (learn the new skill) is key in getting this new information absorbed and ultimately what begins to impact and change our behavior.

Excellent guidelines exist for effective teaching and learning.[8] Specific, best practices for EI training have also been proposed.[9] We propose a few learning principles to guide EI skills training: assessment, guided experience, transfer, ongoing support, and follow-up evaluation.

Assessment

"Why should I be here?" is a question we all ask when we receive any sort of training. It is a good question, and one that good training should address through the wise use of assessments during the training. Good assessment includes time to debrief. It is for this reason that group training sessions often are not the appropriate place for EI ability assessments, given that there is usually insufficient time and privacy to adequately debrief participants.

Guided Experience

"Experience is simply the name we give our mistakes" – Oscar Wilde. Contrary to what many consultants claim, experience itself is a very poor teacher. The reason is that we often learn the wrong lesson from an experience. Uncorrected and unguided experience simply serves to reinforce false beliefs or ineffective behaviors. Consider, for example, the person who continually mis-identifies emotions in others. Although the target people may display nonverbal signals of confusion or disagreement, the observer fails to read, or correctly read, this feedback. Thus, incorrect emotion rules are being reinforced. Therefore, emotionally intelligent training employs experiential exercises that are based on our model, and have adequate participant debriefing so that the lessons can be learned and applied correctly to the learner's world. Case studies and role plays are essential EI skill development tools.

Transfer

Case studies and role plays need to be drawn from the participants' world. This is a relatively easy principle to satisfy through the use of brief, critical incident interviews, or simply by asking people for situations when they were at their emotional worst or emotional best. Participants can also work on a current, difficult situation during the training sessions.

Ongoing Support

You can teach a great deal in a few hours, in a day-long session, or during residential training programs. But what is critical to EI skills training is some ongoing support or coaching. Simple e-mail reminders can be an effective means of keeping the training in front of participants over time. Individual coaching and/or group "refresher" training is also extremely effective.

Follow-Up Evaluation

Did it work? It is a question that researchers ask all the time regarding training but consultants rarely address. That goes for our work, as well: although we always include an evaluative component to training proposals, often clients are just not interested, other than to distribute a rating scale on how much participants got from the training session. A behavioral-based follow-up evaluation is imperative to assess whether a transfer of learning has occurred. In addition, measuring the degree and type of impact regarding the change in behavior on a particular area is essential in the follow-up evaluation.

Emotional Intelligence Training: A Disclaimer

Following the scientist-practitioner model is not easy. As researchers, we are fully aware of the limits that our current knowledge places on our claims. We cannot make wild claims for the efficacy of our training. We have a good deal of anecdotal evidence suggesting that EI skills training is beneficial. We feel confident that these exercises, and our other training techniques, provide people with valuable insights and learning. But we must point out that teaching or enhancing skills may not result in actual increases in measured EI. That is, we make a distinction between one's level of actual EI as measured by an objective assessment such as the

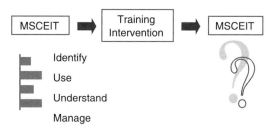

FIGURE 3.1 What would happen to MSCEIT scores after a training program?

Mayer–Salovey–Caruso Emotional Intelligence Test (MSCEIT), and one's everyday EI skills and strategies. As Figure 3.1 illustrates, what exactly would happen to your level of EI, as measured by our objectively-scored ability test of EI, the MSCEIT, if you participated in a rigorous EI-development program? Several research studies are underway to examine this question, but currently we cannot say for certain. Nevertheless, we are writing this chapter because we believe that EI skills training can, and should, be conducted. That is, MSCEIT scores, per se, may or may not increase after a training intervention, but good EI training is likely to have other, positive outcomes, such as enhanced relationships and more frequent prosocial behaviors. Moreover, some individuals may possess a moderate to high EI ability and not actually apply that ability. An EI training program can teach participants how to best apply their individual EI abilities.

Each of the exercises in this chapter is designed to be not just read, but implemented. Transfer of training only occurs if you practice these skills in your environment and apply the learning to your life.

☐ Ability-Based Emotional Intelligence Development Exercises

Exercise 1: Learning Styles and Payoffs

Learning Outcomes

- Assess and analyze your past behavior of learning new skills.
- Forecast your personal payoff to use EI.
- Uncover the personal motivation to develop EI.

Step 1 Instructions

Answer the following three questions about the personal importance of EI to you.

1. Why is EI important to you? Consider . . . What personal importance can you find in EI?
2. How do you intend to use this information?
3. What do you think your personal top three payoffs will be by learning how to use emotions intelligently?

Step 2 Instructions

Answer the following questions regarding how you learn information.

1. When was the last time you learned a new skill? *The skill could be home crafting, tiling, computer software, etc. . . .*
2. What was the skill?
3. What motivated you to learn how to acquire this new skill?
4. What process did you go through to acquire this new skill?
5. What was the most difficult process of learning and using the new skill?
6. What was the easiest part of learning and using the new skill?
7. Looking back, what was the payoff for you to use this new skill? *The payoff could be financial, a sense of pride, accomplishment, helping another, etc.*

Conclusion to Exercise 1

The importance of Exercise 1 is to draw the conclusion that EI is something that we use on a daily, in fact hourly, basis and learning how to improve these skills is as valuable and perhaps even more valuable as other skills that we have learned. For example, if you recently learned how to lay down ceramic tiles you went through the arduous process of learning and perfecting this new skill. You may have used it to tile your kitchen and bathroom and perhaps those of friends or family – if you are really good at it. The skill was useful to help you complete projects. However, you have not needed to use this skill much over the past few months. Unlike tiling, we need to employ our emotional skills each and every day as we take action on our emotions and logical data. It might be worthwhile, therefore, to spend some time developing these critical emotional skills, and then putting them to good use.

Determining what the individual payoff or worth that EI is to you helps to understand its significance in learning this skill. Coming to the realization that you will be using these skills quite often will likely motivate you to want to learn the information and enhance your emotional behavior.

Exercise 2: Basic Emotional Self-Awareness

Learning Outcomes

- Learn an easy method for representing moods and emotions you are experiencing.
- Learn how to track your emotions.

EI Skill: Identify Emotions

Answer these few self-assessment questions prior to beginning this exercise in order to establish greater awareness of this EI skill. Select the answer – a, b or c – that best describes you.

1. Awareness of feelings
   a [ ] I am always aware of how I feel
   b [ ] I am often aware of my feelings
   c [ ] I do not pay much attention to my feelings
2. Express my emotions
   a [ ] My emotional expressions always allow *others* to understand how I feel
   b [ ] Can show some of my emotions
   c [ ] Not good at expressing my emotions
3. Read other people's emotions
   a [ ] Always know others' emotions
   b [ ] Often pick up on others' emotions
   c [ ] Mis-read people's emotions
4. Read subtle, nonverbal emotional cues
   a [ ] Can read between the lines and always pick up on how the person feels
   b [ ] Often read nonverbal cues such as body language
   c [ ] Do not pay much attention to this

Add up your a, b and c responses and record them. Simply, the more "a" responses you have, the more likely it is that you view yourself as emotionally aware and expressive. Read this section to help you better the leverage skills you might possess in emotional identification. If you have more "c" responses, work on this exercise to enhance your skill confidence.

Instructions

As basic as it might seem, the place to begin with clients who need to enhance their identification of emotion in self and others is to teach them that emotions exist and to pay attention to emotions. There are simply a large number of people who do not *look* for emotions, do not notice even the most obvious of clues that are displayed nonverbally or verbally.

How, then, do we begin to discuss a concept such as emotions to a client who might be extremely logical, analytical, and concrete?

- Emotions exist.
- Emotions contain data or information about how you and others are functioning.
- Clues to emotions exist in the world.
- Some emotion clues are easy to spot; others are fleeting and much more subtle.
- Check your perceptions against the context, other clues, with other people, or with the person you are trying to get a better read on.

Mood Meter

To begin the process of asking the question, "how am I feeling," we suggest the use of a very basic tool: the Mood Meter. It is a two-dimensional representation of various feeling states: energy level (from low to high) and emotion (unpleasant or negative to pleasant or positive), each on a ten-point scale. This Mood Meter is shown in Figure 3.2.

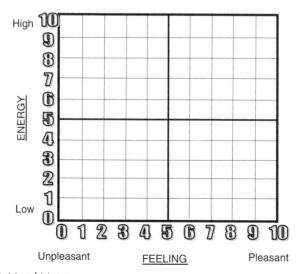

FIGURE 3.2 Mood Meter.

Conclusion to Exercise 2

When a client is ready, it can be helpful to begin to teach a basic form of emotional literacy by matching the energy–emotion grid to emotion or feeling words. We have done this in Figure 3.2.

Once awareness of your own moods and emotions is being enhanced, it is helpful to learn the emotion clues that signal others' emotional states. Although it can seem like a more daunting task, this skill can be easier for some clients to learn than can self-identification of emotion.

Exercise 3: What Does EI Behavior Look Like?

Learning Outcomes

- Understand the four-step Emotional Blueprint.
- Apply the Blueprint to two personal situations.

EI Skill: Identify, Use, Understand, Manage Emotions

Answer these few self-assessment questions prior to beginning this exercise in order to establish greater awareness of this EI skill. Select the answer – a, b or c – that best describes you.

1. I process strong emotions . . .
   a [ ] In order not to exaggerate or minimize them at all times
   b [ ] Much of the time
   c [ ] So as to minimize them and control them
2. I can change a bad mood when required
   a [ ] Almost always
   b [ ] Often
   c [ ] Rarely
3. I stay open to my emotions
   a [ ] Almost always (for all basic emotions)
   b [ ] At times
   c [ ] Rarely
4. My emotions help me to make *better* decisions
   a [ ] Almost always (for all basic emotions)
   b [ ] At times
   c [ ] Rarely

The "a" responses suggest that you are open to emotions, even though you might not find them welcome visitors. This is a key to EI, as emotions contain valuable data about you and the environment. The "c" responses suggest that you are closed off to emotions, or certain emotions at certain times. As a result, you may not have the complete picture.

Instructions

First, read through the two examples of the intelligent and unintelligent use of emotions, and then answer the questions to help you better understand your approach to problem-solving.

Intelligent EI Use

An example of an emotionally intelligent person is Kris. Kris is a nurse who works in a very busy office and is running almost twenty minutes behind seeing her six-year-old patient Alysha. Alysha is scheduled to get a shot. Alysha is accompanied by her mother and waiting in the exam room.

Kris knocks on the door, opens the door, and immediately apologizes for the delay. Kris notices that Alysha is grasping the edge of the exam table with white knuckles and sees that she is scared. She glances over at Alysha's mother and her mother seems fairly content. The mother says "She is just getting a shot today, right?" Kris says, "Yes we will be doing that today." The mother then says "She has done so well with her shots in the past, she is such a trooper."

Kris notices that Alysha is growing more apprehensive and addresses Alysha. She says "So, Alysha, how do you feel about getting this shot today?" Alysha replies with a quivering low voice, "Not so good." Kris says "Why is this shot different then the ones you had in the past? Your Mom says you typically do well." Alysha answers, "Some kids at school were saying the shots this year can make you really sick and die."

Kris then went on to assure Alysha that this particular shot she was getting was not the shot the other kids were talking about and she would be safe receiving the shot. Kris calmed Alysha down and changed Alysha's initial scared emotional state to one that was more accepting.

Kris had a few pieces of information that she picked up on to determine that Alysha's behavior was not that of a normal six-year-old receiving a shot. In fact, if Kris had not taken the time to pick up and address Alysha's emotional behavior and simply chose to administer the shot, Alysha may have become even more terrified after she received the shot. Kris was able to have Alysha leave the doctor's office, although sore in the arm, much calmer than when she went into the office.

The Emotional Blueprint is used to break down how emotions were used intelligently in the above situation. Kris first accurately identified that Alysha was grasping onto the exam table and determined that Alysha was scared. Kris was also able to use what the mother said about her daughter usually being a "trooper" to infer that something had changed between the last shot and this shot.

At the moment before the shot, Kris made the decision to ask Alysha how she felt about getting the shot. Kris knew that having her young patient feeling scared was not normal and Kris wanted to try to calm the young child down. Kris also realized that administering the shot without asking her young patient how she felt was not right. When Alysha replied "not so good" and proceeded to give Kris the reason why she was afraid of the shot, Kris was able to effectively manage the situation with a good outcome for herself, Alysha, and her mother.

Analyzing the Kris example using the Emotional Blueprint gives a better perspective of the four major areas and the information included in those areas.

- *Identify Emotions* – Kris accurately identified that Alysha was scared by recognizing facial expression, body language, and tone of voice.
- *Use Emotions* – Kris could empathize with the scared emotion Alysha was experiencing, and could relate to the apprehension that Alysha felt.
- *Understand Emotions* – Kris knew she needed to move her patient from a scared emotional state to a more relaxed emotion. She did not want to have her patient become more scared or terrified.
- *Manage Emotions* – Kris chose to acknowledge the emotional inform- ation that was displayed and questioned Alysha on how she felt about her shot. She continued to manage Alysha's emotions by assuring her that she would be fine after receiving the shot.

Not So Intelligent EI Use

The obvious choice for Rachel was to go to the Hartt School of Music. Barring that, of course, she should attend the school of music at the University of Connecticut. The decision was based upon irrefutable logic, backed up by a detailed weighted probability model in an Excel spreadsheet. The spreadsheet included almost two dozen critical decision criteria, such as quality of the faculty, residence hall availability, location, graduation rates, course listings, and student body diversity. Each of these factors was given an importance weight. Next, both Rachel and her father evaluated each of the schools she applied to on each of these factors; they compared their ratings and discussed the discrepancies.

The results were clear, but her father wanted to make sure that the results were not due to a fluke in the weights they assigned to each factor, so he also looked at minimum cut-off scores, "must-have" criteria, and a few other decision-making models. While the rankings changed slightly over these multiple methods, there were two clear top choices. Then Rachel dropped the illogical bombshell: she was accepting the offer in Boston, a school ranked much lower on the list, no matter how you sliced the results. Her father concluded that either there was something clearly wrong with her decision making or she did not understand the impressive and elegant evaluation system he had devised for her. He called her to ask "What factor is missing from the list?" and "How did you come up with Boston?" He was truly mystified. "Everything is in the list, and I agree with all of our ratings and numbers," Rachel replied. "But I just *liked* Boston the best." Her father was aghast. After all, the whole point of the logical approach to college decision making was to avoid these subjective judgments. He asked her, "Was the weather that nice the day you visited, or was the tour guide especially friendly?" He was reminded that they had trudged through drifting snow the day of the campus visit and that the tour guide was spectacularly uninformed. Now, he began to be quite concerned about Rachel and her irrational behavior.

But was it irrational? Was her decision an intelligent decision, or one based on unreliable feelings? It is true that her decision was emotion-based, but also that it was an intelligent decision. It is also true that the father's decision-making process was faultless from a logical, rational point of view – and, his decision was also quite wrong (although we hesitate to call it an unintelligent decision). The father's decision-making process was incomplete – it did not include data that can be obtained from one's feelings. Rachel's feeling that Boston was a place where she could be challenged, learn, and enjoy was hard to quantify, and anyway, asking a question about how a school decision "feels" would not fit into a logical decision-making model. Her feeling that the decision was the right one was based on a number of factors, and her internal review of logical factors supported the wisdom of this feeling. That is, Rachel did consider whether the positive feeling she got in Boston was due to some extraneous, non-data driven factor, and she wisely and correctly concluded that it was not.

The dad in this story failed to consider, or to integrate, the data of emotions in his decision-making process. Perhaps he simply did not trust his feelings, or his daughter's, or perhaps he was unaware of the overall feelings-based evaluation of various schools. Either way, this is an example of an emotionally unintelligent decision. It is interesting to note that several years after this college decision was made Rachel is indeed thriving in the environment she selected, and her father claims that he will not repeat his logical error the next time.

Activity Questions and Conclusions to Exercise 3

Consider a decision you made recently which ended up being a *bad* decision. The rational data you had available supported your decision, but you felt somewhat uncomfortable about the decision. However, you ignored your gut feeling and went with the logical decision. It turned out that this was also the *wrong* decision. Answer the following questions about this situation:

1. What was the situation?
2. What were the feelings you experienced?
3. Were you aware of these feelings at the time?
4. If so, what did you attribute them to, or how did you manage them?
5. In retrospect, what were the feelings suggesting?

Next, consider a decision you have made which was a *good* decision, one where you went with your gut feel, much as Rachel did in the story above, and answer the same set of questions.

1. What was the situation?
2. What were the feelings you experienced?
3. Were you aware of these feelings at the time?
4. If so, what did you attribute them to, or how did you manage them?
5. In retrospect, what were the feelings suggesting?

One aspect of managing emotions is to be able to stay open to feelings, even though they might be unwelcome. If emotions contain data, then it will often be foolhardy to ignore such data.

Exercise 4: An Emotional Blueprint Case Study

Learning Outcomes

* Identify the four components of the Emotional Blueprint.
* Learn how emotions impact our behavior and decision making.
* Understand how EI is a balance of both facts and emotion.

EI Skill: Identify, Use, Understand, Manage Emotions

Answer these few self-assessment questions prior to beginning this exercise in order to establish greater awareness of this EI skill. Select the answer – a, b or c – that best describes you.

1. I pay attention to hunches, instinct, or gut feel
   a [ ] Almost always

b [ ] Often
c [ ] Rarely
2. I am aware of how my emotions influence me
   a [ ] Almost always
   b [ ] Often
   c [ ] Rarely
3. My hunches pay off
   a [ ] Almost always
   b [ ] At times
   c [ ] Rarely
4. Uncomfortable feelings lead me to review my conclusions and decision-making process
   a [ ] Almost always (for all major decisions)
   b [ ] At times
   c [ ] Rarely

Do you "go with your gut feel" or do you rely on logic and reason? It may not be smart to go with your instinct if your instinct is wrong. Thus, "a" responses indicate that you go with your gut feel, but they do not necessarily mean that this is a good thing! However, the "c" responses often point to a lack of emotional insight.

Instructions

Read the case study and answer the questions at the end of the study.

Larry is a detective who is in court waiting to have his case called by the District Attorney. While Larry is waiting in the courtroom he is watching a different case being discussed. Although Larry soon realizes that the case being argued before him is part of his police district, he is unfamiliar with the specific details of this case. But as he is hearing the attorneys discuss the case with the judge, Larry has a gut feel that some members of the department he belongs to do not have all the facts gathered to present to the court, and that this lack of knowledge could impact the integrity of the case and the outcome. Larry also senses that there is more to this story than is being shared by his fellow officers.

   The case he is hearing involves several teenagers who were accused of assault and battery on another teenager. The case seems fairly straightforward when the father of the alleged victim stands up and calmly says "Your honor, I would like to speak, may I?" The judge grants permission to the father and the father quietly addresses the court: "This is not just typical kids fighting. Your honor, my son was targeted and beat up because he is gay. I believe that this is a hate crime." The judge rules that the case be continued pending the collection and presentation of additional information. Larry, the observing detective, immediately walks over to the District Attorney and says "If there is anything I can do to help further investigate this case, please let me know and I will take care of it."

Case Study Questions

Step 1. Answer the following five questions in this case study.
Step 2. Fill in each of the blanks below the questions with what you have learned about Larry's story and the Emotional Blueprint.

1. What do you think motivated the detective to address the district attorney?
2. What was the detective likely feeling when he heard the case before him?
3. What do you think were the detective's goals for addressing the District Attorney?
4. Do you think the detective's actions may help to produce a positive outcome in this case?
5. If the father had not stood up and presented his information, would this have affected the detective's actions?

Like many of the cases we present, this case is based on a true story, so we can share with you what actually occurred and what the real answers are.

1. The detective was motivated for two reasons. The facts of the case were not pulled together properly and he was moved by the father's statement regarding his son.
2. The detective said he was surprised at the information the father presented and felt sympathetic to the father and the victim. He also felt that there was injustice because the case was not given a thorough investigation to present all the necessary facts for a proper case hearing.
3. Larry wanted to participate in getting this case presented properly.
4. Yes! Compiling the facts that were missing will help to have all the information be heard.
5. Yes! Larry stated he would not have approached the District Attorney if the father had not stood up and so calmly expressed what he believed had happened to his son.

Conclusion

Larry acted on the emotional and factual information that was presented before him at the trial. The goal of this activity is to see the relevance of both logical data and emotional data and apply this story to the Emotional Blueprint. By Larry's own admission, given the facts alone of the weak case, he would have not have involved himself. Unknowingly, Larry went through the steps of the Emotional Blueprint.

Larry knew that the facts of the case were not adequately compiled. However, the pure facts, or in this case lack thereof, were not motivating enough for him to get involved. He further elaborated that it was the father's tone of voice, spoken so calmly and with strong conviction, that inspired him to approach the District Attorney. He said the emotion he felt while the father was speaking was proud. He was proud of the father because he felt the father was taking a huge normative social risk by letting the courtroom know of his son's sexual orientation.

Exercise 5: Emotional Experiences

Learning Outcomes

• Assess our emotional tendencies for greater self-awareness.
• Increase emotional understanding.

EI Skill: Use Emotions

Read each question and then select the answer – a, b or c – that best describes you.

1. Can generate an emotion
   a [ ] Yes, for *all* basic emotions
   b [ ] For many emotions
   c [ ] Rarely, or with difficulty
2. Influence of emotions on my thinking:
   a [ ] Emotions always focus me on what is important
   b [ ] Emotions have some impact on me
   c [ ] Emotions distract me
3. I feel what others feel . . .
   a [ ] Almost always
   b [ ] Usually
   c [ ] Rarely
4. When someone describes a powerful emotional event . . .
   a [ ] I feel what they feel for *all* emotions
   b [ ] My feelings change a bit
   c [ ] My feelings generally stay the same

Are you the emotional, sensitive type, or the tough, John Wayne sort of person? The more "c" responses you gave yourself, the more you lean toward the John Wayne style. There is a time and a place for the steely-eyed stare of a John Wayne, but in many interpersonal situations it helps to feel for others, to "get inside their heads" in order to better understand their perspective.

Instructions

Listed below are ten behaviors. Consider each item and indicate the frequency with which you experience each of these behaviors.

Never	Once a Year	A Few Times Each Year	Monthly	Weekly	Daily	Several Times Daily
1	2	3	4	5	6	7

1. Clenched jaw and may feel warm or hot _____
2. Warm and balanced feeling _____
3. Open mouth and eyes wide _____
4. Sneer and thinking self superior _____
5. Head to one side, leaning forward _____
6. Use finger and point out flaws in others _____
7. Sigh and feel as if you have had enough, possibly shut down

    _____

8. Open and agreeable, feel warm and light _____
9. Heart beats faster, cool feeling in body, and negative thoughts

    _____

10. Feel "blue," sluggish, and easily get down _____

Conclusion to Exercise 5

This list links various emotions to feeling states. Some of us are more aware of our physical feelings, and are more accurate reporting feelings than we are emotions. That is, when asked how we "feel," we struggle for the exact emotion term. Reflection and greater awareness come about when we are not asked to label the emotions experienced, but instead to label the physical sensations and feelings. We may also not acknowledge or access certain emotions which may be uncomfortable for us. Some people shy away from happiness and others may not use or want to use anger. This activity helps us first to see the behavior of that emotion and then correctly label the emotion. Learning how to manage emotions involves being open to emotional information. The next activity helps us to gain further self-awareness of our typical emotional lens versus the emotional lens we would like to convey or use.

Exercise 6: Feelings and Emotions

Learning Outcomes

• Match physical feelings to their correct emotion label.

EI Skill: Use and Understand Emotions

Again, quickly read each question and then select the answer – a, b or c – that best describes you.

1. I feel things deeply
   a [ ] Almost always
   b [ ] Usually
   c [ ] Rarely
2. I can describe my feelings and emotions
   a [ ] Almost always
   b [ ] Usually
   c [ ] Rarely
3. My range of feelings is
   a [ ] Extremely broad and deep
   b [ ] Broad
   c [ ] Somewhat limited
4. I have a wide range of feelings
   a [ ] Very much
   b [ ] Somewhat
   c [ ] No, not really

Some of us feel things deeply, but not for the full range of emotions. The "a" responses indicate that you feel a wide range of emotions. If this describes you, the following exercise can help you to leverage this ability. Those of us endorsing "c" responses can use the exercise to push beyond our existing feelings-based limits.

Instructions

Return to the list of ten behaviors. Only this time, try to come up with the emotion term that best describes these feelings. Do this on your own. If you struggle trying to come up with a one-word descriptor, take your best guess. If you still are having trouble, then refer to the list below for help. We will give you the answers later in the chapter.

Clenched jaw and may feel warm or hot _____
Warm and balanced feeling _____
Open mouth and eyes wide _____
Sneer and thinking self superior _____
Head to one side, leaning forward _____
Use finger and point out flaws in others _____
Sigh and feel as if you have had enough, possibly shut down _____
Open and agreeable, feel warm and light _____
Heart beats faster, cool feeling in body, and negative thoughts _____
Feel "blue," sluggish, and easily get down _____

Helpful Hints: Possible Emotion Terms:
Anger
Annoyance
Contempt
Disgust
Excitement
Fear
Happiness
Interest
Rage
Sadness
Surprise

Conclusion to Exercise 6

This activity helps us to begin to correctly label the emotion associated with that behavior. Expanding our emotional vocabulary is a key component in learning how to use emotions intelligently. The Answer Key is given in Figure 3.3. Let us see how many you got right!

Answer Key

1. Anger
2. Content
3. Surprise
4. Contempt
5. Interest
6. Anger
7. Frustrated
8. Happy
9. Fear
10. Sadness

FIGURE 3.3 Exercise Answer Key.

Exercise 7: Energy of Emotions

Learning Outcomes

• Understand causes of basic emotions.
• Learn how emotions impact thinking and behavior.

EI Skill: Understand Emotions

Try this set of four questions before starting the next exercise.

1. My emotional vocabulary is . . .
   a [ ] Highly differentiated and rich
   b [ ] About average
   c [ ] Not very large
2. My understanding of why people feel the way they do usually yields . . .
   a [ ] Excellent insights
   b [ ] Some insight
   c [ ] Some missing pieces
3. My emotional what-if thinking yields . . .
   a [ ] 100% accurate prediction of actions
   b [ ] At times able to predict feelings
   c [ ] Tend to not project how people will feel
4. When I try to determine what causes emotions, I . . .
   a [ ] Am able to understand the causes of all basic emotions
   b [ ] Usually link the emotion to a cause
   c [ ] Sometimes make the connection

It is difficult to understand something if you lack precise terms. Complex emotional vocabulary and accurate emotional what-if analyses, indicated by "a" responses, are necessary for emotionally intelligent decision making.

Background

Have you ever wondered why when you are in a really good mood and feeling alive and energetic you can suddenly get angry when something bothers you? Emotions follow rules and emotions also have patterns of energy. For instance, when one is experiencing low energy, emotions in this low-energy category include contentment, sadness, or even boredom.

So, getting back to our question. You are in a happy and energetic mood and something bothers you, let us say you feel as if something completely and totally unfair had happened right at the moment you were so happily experiencing that positive emotion. You suddenly become angry and start raising your voice to that poor unsuspecting person who delivered you the upsetting news. At that point, you realize, "wait a minute . . . I wasn't in a bad mood, why am I now so angry?"

Blame it on the rules of emotions and your high energy level. It takes energy to be angry and it takes energy to be excited and happy. Let us take another example of when you are in a happy mood. You are joyously going about your day, feeling tremendous, and you decide you want to go outside for a jog. You change into your workout clothes, put on your sneakers, and before you leave you turn on the television to catch a glimpse of the weather forecast before your jog. Then you suddenly see on the television that a devastating natural disaster has occurred and may have killed hundreds of people. You are shocked by the news and soon you become tearful as you watch the reporter interview people who cannot find their missing loved ones. At this moment, you are likely to be sad.

Your energy level is not the same as it was before you saw the television report. Prior to the report, you were positive, happy, feeling energetic, and ready for a workout. After seeing the devastating news, your energy has down-shifted and now you find you have little energy to go for that jog.

It is important to recognize the process of emotions and that emotions follow rules. By better understanding these rules, we can more effectively navigate through what is often perceived as muddy waters or soft skills.

Emotional Causes, Thinking, and Behaviors

One of the most instructional of graphics is the one based upon Plutchik's[10] circumplex model of emotions. We have adapted that graphic in Figure 3.4 to illustrate the six basic emotions, three levels of intensity for each emotion, an exemplar of each emotion expression, and the influence that the emotion has on thinking. This graphic helps to illustrate that many different emotions exist, that combinations of certain emotions form other emotions, and illustrates the intensity or energy level of emotions compared to each other. For example, happy is similar to joyous, but the emotion of joy is at a higher intensity or energy level than is happy.

We take this work a step further and clarify how feeling a certain emotion affects our thinking, which then impacts our behavior and describes the cause of that respective emotion. The chart opposite helps to emphasize this area.

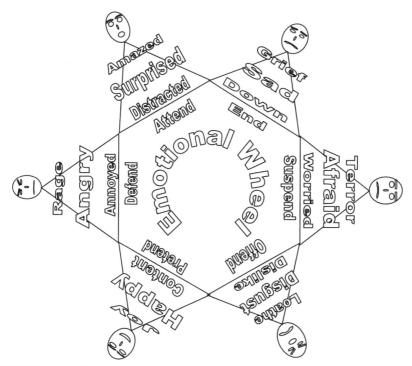

FIGURE 3.4 Basic emotions, influence on thinking, level of intensity, and facial expression.

Instructions

Review the chart below to understand emotions, causes, and the physical and thinking behavior associated with those emotions.

Emotion	Cause	Physical Behavior	Thinking Behavior
Sad	Lost something	Slow and facial expressions turned downward	Low motivation
Happy	Gained something	Energetic and facial expressions turned upward	Open to new ideas, agreeable
Angry	Something unfair	Clenched teeth and sharp eyebrows	Negative and unpleasant thoughts
Surprised	Something unexpected	Open mouth, wide eyes	Thinking is halted for a brief moment
Afraid	Possible threat	Trembling, staying in place	Consider ways to exit the situation or protect self
Disgusted	Something unpalatable	Wrinkled nose	Reject whatever it is that creates the emotion

Now, take a few minutes to complete the chart for yourself. In other words, consider what makes you feel sad, or the last time you felt sad. What caused this emotion? How did you behave when feeling sad? And how did the experience of this emotion influence your thinking?

Emotion	What Causes You to Feel This Way?	Your Physical Behavior	Your Thinking Behavior
Sad			
Happy			
Angry			
Surprised			
Afraid			
Disgusted			

Conclusion to Exercise 7

Charts or tables are an effective way to explain and view information. However, they are not necessarily a good way to ensure that the learner has actually worked through the material to comprehend and process the information presented in the chart. The following activity helps the learner to think through the causes, physical sensations, and thoughts associated with certain emotions. This can also heighten a learner's level of self-awareness.

Exercise 8: Emotional Lenses

Learning Outcomes

• Learn about the impact of emotional filters, or emotional lenses.
• Understand our individual emotional lenses by analyzing the sequence of emotions, causes, and behavior.

EI Skill: Manage Emotions

Reflect on these four questions before starting the next exercise.

1. I can tell what irks people
   a [ ] All the time for most people
   b [ ] Most of the time
   c [ ] Some of the time
2. I perceive when others' perceptions are clear or mistaken
   a [ ] All the time

 b [ ] Most of the time
 c [ ] Some of the time
3. I understand what motivates others' behavior
 a [ ] All the time
 b [ ] Most of the time
 c [ ] Some of the time
4. I am aware of how people's moods impact them
 a [ ] Always
 b [ ] Usually
 c [ ] Often

"Insight" can mean many different things. In this case, "a" responses indicate that you have a developed sense of emotional insight; "c" responses suggest that you are not sure about your insight into how people feel, and what motivates or affects them.

Background

An interesting way to look at how emotions affect our thinking is to consider a colored lens over your eye. Each different color represents an emotion, as shown in Figure 3.5. Let us call these emotional lenses. Emotional lenses are the lenses that we have in our mind and feel in our body that cause us to view situations in a particular way. Sometimes these emotional lenses are helpful and accurate and other times they are harmful and off target to the situation at hand.

To illustrate this point, imagine a ring of different colored lenses. Each colored lens represents an emotion. The red lens represents anger, the blue lens sadness, the yellow lens happiness, and the orange lens concern. This next part will take some visual imagery. When the lens is put in front

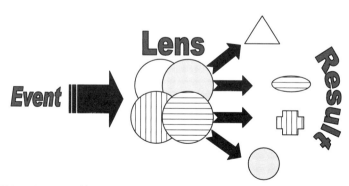

FIGURE 3.5 Emotional lenses.

of your eye you feel that emotion and you also think in accordance with that emotion.

Let us take two people, Sammy and Maria. Sammy has experienced a great deal of tragedy in a short period of time and she is down and out. As a result she has not gone out of her way to reach out to her close friend Maria. Sammy's lens is blue, which is sadness. Her friend Maria has a red lens of anger. Maria is upset because Sammy has not contacted her in a few weeks. As a result Maria wrote Sammy a letter in which she let out her angry feelings towards Sammy.

A few questions are important to ask. Are Sammy's feelings justified? Are Maria's feelings justified? Does Sammy or Maria have a tendency to lean toward certain emotions and not others? Let us assume that Sammy's feelings are justified; the recent tragic events in her life would put anyone in a sad mood.

Figure 3.6 outlines the different stages experienced by Sammy and Maria. They are not feeling the same emotion, which is affecting their ability to successfully communicate and ultimately maintain their good friendship.

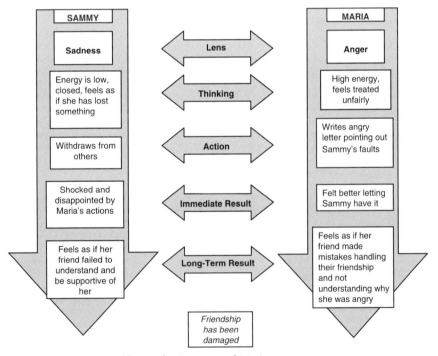

FIGURE 3.6 Emotional lenses for Sammy and Maria.

Now consider an alternative emotional lens and see how the situation between Sammy and Maria plays out. Keep in mind, Maria's emotional lens is now no longer one of "anger" but of interest or concern because Sammy has not contacted her in an unusually long period of time. Figure 3.7 shows the alternative ending to this situation.

Conclusion to Exercise 8

Exercise 8 serves three main purposes. The first is to have the learner understand the impact of emotions and behavior through a visual chart of Sammy and Maria's emotions and actions for a particular situation. The second is to recognize that by having the emotional lens of anger change to a different emotional lens of concern yields different results. The third is to have the learner analyze an especially challenging situation by creating a similar flow chart and through creating this chart the learner can determine which emotional lens is best to use for their challenging situation.

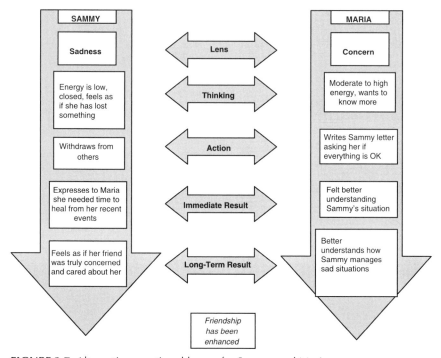

FIGURE 3.7 Alternative emotional lenses for Sammy and Maria.

Exercise 9: Emotion Lens Personal Application

Learning Outcomes

- Understand the process flow of emotional information and its impact on thinking and behavior.
- Increase self-awareness by applying the emotional lens exercise to a personal situation.
- Better gauge emotional tendencies for yourself and others.
- Learn to use specific emotions to match situational outcomes.
- Begin to manage and forecast relational outcomes by using EI.

EI Skill: Manage Emotions

Reflect on these four questions before starting the next exercise.

1. I know what "sets me off"
   a [ ] All the time
   b [ ] Most of the time
   c [ ] Some of the time
2. My perceptions are typically unclouded and clear
   a [ ] All the time
   b [ ] Most of the time
   c [ ] Some of the time
3. I understand what motivates my behavior
   a [ ] All the time
   b [ ] Most of the time
   c [ ] Some of the time
4. I am aware of how my moods impact me
   a [ ] Always
   b [ ] Usually
   c [ ] Often

We can understand other people, but do we understand ourselves? Selecting "a" responses to this set of questions indicates that you feel you know yourself. Selecting more "c" than "a" responses indicates otherwise. If you are more of a "c" person, attend carefully to this next exercise.

Instructions

Step 1. Consider a recent conflict situation with a friend, colleague, co-worker, employee, supervisor, etc., where the outcome of the interaction was not what you would have wanted and may even have left you or the other person feeling poorly. Use Figures 3.8 and 3.9, as well as the questions below, to help guide you through this activity.

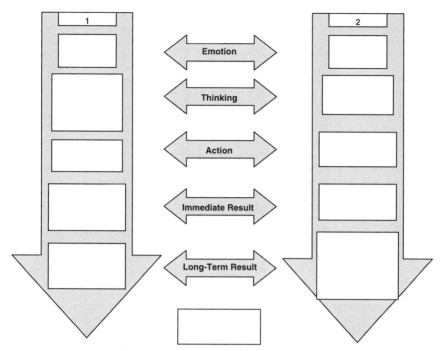

FIGURE 3.8 Emotional Lens Personal Application.

1. Describe the nature of the situation.
2. Who was involved?
3. Identify the emotional lenses used by the participants in the conflict.
4. Describe as well as possible the other individuals involved.
5. How did emotions impact your thinking?
6. How did emotions impact the other individuals' thinking?
7. What was the result?

Step 2. Now, let us consider your ideal result. Answer the following questions and use Figure 3.9 to learn how to manage the situation for the ideal result.

1. What is your ideal result?
2. What emotional lenses need to change for you and perhaps the other person to produce this result?
3. What is the emotional payoff and payoff in general for this ideal result?

Conclusion to Exercise 9

The goal of this exercise is to take a real and personal situation and outline the process steps from beginning to end to see how the emotional lenses

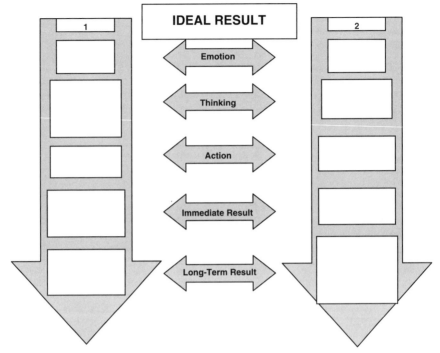

FIGURE 3.9 Emotional Lens Personal Application: Ideal result.

of the individuals involved affect the outcome of the situation. Different emotional lenses affect how we take in information, process that information, and subsequently act on the information. By being open and adjusting your emotional lens, you may be able to obtain different and more desired results.

Exercise 10: Transforming; Influencing, and Using EI

Learning Outcomes

- Learn what emotions generate the best modes of thinking.
- Understand how to better access your personal emotional range to influence others.
- Manage your emotions.

EI Skill: Use and Manage Emotions

Reflect on these four questions before starting the next exercise.

1. I know how moods influence thinking and behavior
   a [ ] All of the time for all basic emotions
   b [ ] Most of the time
   c [ ] Some of the time
2. I match my mood to the task at hand
   a [ ] All the time
   b [ ] Most of the time
   c [ ] Some of the time
3. My moods help me
   a [ ] All the time
   b [ ] Most of the time
   c [ ] Some of the time
4. I get people into the "right" mood
   a [ ] Always
   b [ ] Usually
   c [ ] Often

Moods influence thinking. That can be smart, or not, depending upon what sort of mood, and whether it enhances the thinking you need to engage in or not. The "a" responses assume that you know how moods and thinking interact, and how to match the right mood to the right task.

Background

How do we move from one emotional state to another? How do we know what emotions to feel that produce the best outcome for situations? How do we influence others to achieve our desired results? The last part of the chapter is dedicated to transforming and using EI. Now that we have the basis of information that emotions impact our thinking and behavior and that different emotional lenses produce different outcomes, we can begin to transform ourselves to influence others and use emotions interpersonally.

When you truly "feel" an emotion, there is a physical change that occurs in your body. As a result, your facial expression may change, your tone may change, body posture may change, and a person's thinking is altered. If we are to influence others, then we need to get the "influen-cees" thinking differently also by having the other person feel the targeted emotion we would like for them to experience. After all, the definition of influence is "to affect the nature, development, or condition of; modify." Being able to modify the emotions of others is a crucial component of knowing how to utilize emotional information.

Influencing others – an example

Kevin is a hard working, smart, analytical, and meticulous engineer for a high-tech company. Kevin wants to convince a friend of his to start a new business venture. Although Kevin's friend, Paul, is even more analytical than Kevin and not much of a risk taker, Kevin decides he will approach Paul while they are about to engage in one of their favorite pastimes. Kevin realizes that he needs Paul to be open to hearing about this opportunity and does not want Paul to ask him all the details of the business plan as he does not have the full details around the plan just yet. Kevin plans on addressing Paul during the drive to the football stadium.

Kevin decides he wants Paul to be excited about the opportunity. If he can get Paul excited about the concept of the new business venture and less focused on highlighting all the many risks to start a business, then he might have a shot at engaging Paul. Kevin also realizes that he himself needs to feel the excited emotion and to approach Paul in an enthusiastic manner. The mood is already set to be positive as they are en route to the football stadium and they always have a great time driving to the game together.

The example of Kevin illustrates that he had a specific goal in mind with Paul. He wanted Paul to be enthusiastic about entering into a new business venture. He knew that if he approached Paul during work hours, he would likely go into the many reasons why the business would not work, versus approaching him when he was in a light and jovial mood. Kevin's next step with Paul is to feel the enthusiasm about the business venture as he explains it to Paul and have Paul also feel the enthusiasm. Influencing others can also be labeled as emotional contagion. Emotional contagion is when we feel an emotion and influence others around us for them to also feel that respective emotion.

The following chart, adapted from Reference 4, helps to illustrate how emotions can be used for influencing others.

Step / Process	What It Is	Helpful Ways to Feel
Idea Generation		
"Blue-Sky" Thinking	What if you had no restraints?	Happy
Brainstorming	Use associations that rise with certain objects	Happy
Idea Evaluation		
Fault Seeking	Consider possible problems, and what *could* go wrong	Somewhat afraid
Goal Matching	Match the goals of the project to features of the idea	Neutral mood

Step / Process	What It Is	Helpful Ways to Feel
Idea Selection		
Checklist	Assign weight to each aspect of the goal and each idea	Neutral mood
Implementation		
Group Consensus	Get buy-in from team	Happy and interested
Develop Action Plan	Specific steps, resources, timing, and responsible party	Interested
Take Action	Begin implementation	Happy and excited
Follow-Up	Monitor progress, make adjustments, stay on task, and achieve the desired outcome	Negative mood to evaluate possible issues. Happy and positive mood to stay motivated and overcome anticipated and unanticipated obstacles

Instructions: Getting YOU in the Mood!

Step 1. Listed below are four emotions. Think of a time when you felt these emotions. The goal is to have you go back and actually feel these emotions. Take one emotion at a time. Use these questions/guidelines to assist you.

1. Think of what led up to you feeling that emotion.
2. Describe the sights, sounds, energy, in the experience.
3. Describe the situation in full detail as if you are preparing yourself to tell the story to another individual.

Emotions

1. Enthusiastic
2. Interested
3. Apprehensive
4. Trusting

Getting THEM in the mood!

Can you influence another individual to have them feel a certain emotion?

Step 2. Use your personal situation in Exercise 9 and answer the following questions.

1. What is your desired outcome?
2. What emotional state do you need to be in?

3. What state do you want the other person to be in?
4. What can you do to bring yourself in that state?
5. What can you do to influence the other person to be in that state? Think of statements, questions, and consider the environment and the typical emotional mood of the person.

Conclusion to Exercise 10

The final aspect of using emotions to influence others is to actually have the other person feel the emotion. This requires an understanding of what emotions are, how they impact thinking, and the self-awareness necessary for us to be genuine in correctly identifying our own emotional state. Knowing what puts you and others in the mood is a great start; actually putting yourself and others in those states is the transformational aspect of EI.

A little emotional planning can go a long way. Sometimes the feelings and emotions we bring to a situation are helpful, and sometimes they are not. You can opt out of that situation if the mood is not just right, or you can try to change the mood to better match the needs of the situation.

☐ Conclusion

The goal of these activities was to have the learner become more aware of how they learn new skills, to become more familiar with the role of emotions, to gain new insight and self-awareness in their own emotional tendencies, and to apply EI analysis to a personal challenge. The outcome of these exercises should be that you acquire or enhance a few of your emotional skills, but such learning involves more than merely reading these exercises; learning and change require effort, so you actually need to implement these exercises, on a number of occasions, over a long period of time. Some of the ideas may work for you, and others may not. You may have dismissed some of the exercises after a cursory scan, but if so we ask that you return to that exercise and give it a try. Some person, somewhere, has benefited from each of these exercises in this chapter, and so perhaps you will too. That mild discomfort you felt when you read the exercise might be a clue, a hint, a bit of data. The data may suggest that this is an area that will stress you, but also challenge you. (Of course, that uncomfortable feeling can also result from a poor piece of writing, or a faulty instructional design, but let us stick with the first causal factor.)

The key to emotional intelligence is realizing that there is a balance of logic and emotion. We need to have a clear realization that we, in fact, can use emotions intelligently. This takes knowledge about emotions, self-awareness, and the motivation to want to change our thinking, which will change our behavior.

This chapter began with the story about two types of Sneetches: emotion-based Sneetches and logic-based Sneetches. Neither sort of Sneetch is preferred over the other, and both perspectives are important to consider. A blending of the two Sneetch approaches yields EI behavior. However, this analogy applies only to our view of the role of emotions in thinking, rather than to the actual way that humans are wired. Instead, perhaps we are more like Dorothy in *The Wizard of Oz* who possesses all she needs to return home to Kansas but is unaware of this power.

☐ Acknowledgments

Some of the exercises and assessments were adapted from other sources, including our one-day EI training workshops. Thanks to Josh Freedman for the Dr. Seuss reference.

☐ References

1. Bechara, A., Tranel, D., & Damasio, A. R. (2000). Poor judgment in spite of high intellect: Neurological evidence for emotional intelligence. In R. Bar-On & J. D. A. Parker (Eds.), *The handbook of emotional intelligence: Theory, development, assessment, and application at home, school, and in the workplace* (pp. 192–214). San Francisco: Jossey-Bass.
2. Wilson, T. D., Lisle, D. J., Schooler, J. W., Hodges, S. D., et al. (1993). Introspecting about reasons can reduce post-choice satisfaction. *Personality and Social Psychology Bulletin, 19*, 331–339.
3. Mayer, J. D., & Salovey, P. (1997) What is emotional intelligence? In P. Salovey & D. Sluyter (Eds.), *Emotional development and emotional intelligence: Implications for educators* (pp. 3–31). New York: Basic Books.
4. Caruso, D. R., & Salovey, P. (2004). *The emotionally intelligent manager.* San Francisco: Jossey-Bass.
5. Caruso, D. R., Mayer, J. D., & Salovey, P. (2002). Emotional intelligence and emotional leadership. In R. E. Riggio, S. E. Murphy, & F. J. Pirozzolo (Eds.), *Multiple intelligences and leadership* (pp. 55–74). Mahwah, NJ: Lawrence Erlbaum Associates, Inc.
6. Lopes, P. N., Salovey, P., & Straus, R. (2003). Emotional intelligence, personality, and the perceived quality of social relationships. *Personality and Individual Differences, 35*, 641–658.
7. Rosete, D., & Ciarrochi, J. (2005). Emotional intelligence and its relationship to workplace performance outcomes of leadership effectiveness. *Leadership and Organization Development Journal, 26*, 388–399.
8. Halpern, D. F., & Hakel, M. D. (2002). *Applying the science of learning to the university and beyond. New directions for teaching and learning.* San Francisco: Jossey-Bass.
9. Cherniss, C., Goleman, D., Emmerling, R., Cowan, K., & Adler, M. (1998). *Guidelines for best practice,* available at www.eiconsortium.org/research/guidelines.htm

10. Plutchik, R. (1980). A general psychoevolutionary theory of emotion. In R. Plutchik & H. Kellerman (Eds.), *Emotion: Theory, research, and experience: Vol. 1. Theories of emotion* (pp. 3–33). New York: Academic Press.

Joseph Ciarrochi
John Blackledge
Linda Bilich
Virginia Bayliss

4

CHAPTER

Improving Emotional Intelligence: A Guide to Mindfulness-Based Emotional Intelligence Training

For millennia, human beings have used language to facilitate the creation of increasingly sophisticated technology. Language has allowed the creation of medicines to combat disease and prolong life, houses to provide protection from the elements, and the invention of a nearly countless variety of machines that work to make our lives easier.

Yet while language has had a profound effect on prolonging life and enhancing material comfort, it has done relatively little to alleviate psychological suffering. Research suggests that approximately 33% of people have a diagnosable mental disorder, and over 50% of us seriously contemplate suicide at some point in our lives.[1] While language has allowed us to conquer the planet, explore the stars, surgically transplant organs, and cure a variety of medical diseases, it has also "stood watch" while the numbers of commonly recognized psychiatric diagnoses have increased dramatically from 106 to 365 in the past five decades[2,3] and as we have developed increasingly inventive and efficient ways to wage war and kill one another. Despite all our comforts and material wealth, we do not seem to be any happier.[4]

There is something very peculiar about the human animal. Contrasted to domestic animals such as dogs and cats, which by all accounts appear "happy" simply if they are fed, watered, kept warm, and not beaten, human beings have the all-too-commonly observed ability to suffer psychologically even when their basic needs are met. We fear the future, regret the past, know that we and all those we love will eventually die, and find increasingly inventive ways to be dissatisfied with objectively "fine" circumstances – afflictions our animal friends have not been evidenced to share.

What if it is no coincidence that language has borne witness not only to the dramatic evolution of technology, but also to a legacy of human suffering that appears unparalleled in our non-human counterparts? Specifically, what if language's ability to allow categorization and evaluation of our experiences – at the core of our ability to invent and refine – also is directly responsible for our ability to categorize and evaluate our experiences in ways that make us miserable? And more importantly, if language processes do play an important role in enhancing human suffering, what can we do about it? We intend to summarize an intervention with considerable empirical support designed to address this very feature of language in the pages that follow, and to describe briefly how this intervention is theorized to work. However, to allow these issues to be discussed with clarity, we must first present a few relevant definitions.

Definitions

Emotional intelligence (EI) refers to people's ability to process emotions and deal effectively with them, that is, it refers to people's *potential*. In contrast, "emotionally intelligent behavior (EIB)" refers to how effectively people actually behave in the presence of emotions and emotionally charged thoughts. Our chapter will focus on EIB.

Simply put, emotionally unintelligent behavior occurs when emotions and thoughts impede effective action, and emotionally intelligent behavior occurs when emotions and thoughts do not impede effective action, or when they facilitate effective action. Emotional intelligence (as an ability) is one set of processes hypothesized to promote emotionally intelligent behavior. There are other potential processes, many of which will be discussed in this chapter.

Perhaps a few examples of EIB will clarify our definition. If you are anxious, does that feeling stop you from socializing (we assume this would be inconsistent with your goal of meeting new people)? If you are very angry at your friend, do you hit him (assuming your goal is to maintain friendly relations)? If you feel sad, does this stop you from caring for a loved one (assuming you value such "care")? These are three examples of emotionally unintelligent behavior. The interventions that we describe in this chapter are hypothesized to help people act more intelligently and more effectively pursue their personal values and goals when they feel anxious, angry, sad, or a variety of other unpleasant emotions. According to our model, EIB is presumed to reduce unnecessary suffering. Thus, reduced suffering can essentially be viewed as an after-effect of people moving toward what they value (or engaging in EIB).

☐ A Brief Overview of the Theory Underlying Mindfulness-Based Emotional Intelligence Training: Fusion, Avoidance, and Relational Frame Theory

The theory underlying Mindfulness-Based Emotional Intelligence Training (MBEIT) can be a bit difficult to understand and may not seem of direct relevance to applied settings. However, it is important to note that the intervention we will describe is grounded in the basic experimental theory presented in this section, and that this theory describes precisely how language gains (and loses) the ability to enhance psychological distress and disable effective action. While it is certainly possible to skip these next few paragraphs and simply read the intervention section, this theoretical discussion is intended to enhance your coherent conceptual understanding of the intervention that follows.

Relational Frame Theory (RFT) has been used to account for language's ability to enhance suffering and facilitate ineffective action. It has been tested in research several dozen times under highly controlled conditions, and has found substantial experimental support during the last two decades.[5] Research on RFT has made a number of consistent findings about the nature of human language relevant to our discussion in this chapter.

Principle 1: Language Changes Experience

Research has shown that language is bidirectionally related to experience.[5] For example, focusing your attention on the word "milk" for several moments will likely make some of the features of actual milk (its color, taste, texture, and so on) psychologically present. Less benignly, attending closely to a phrase like "I'm dying" will likely elicit a degree of the anxiety experienced when death is impending – even though, for most of us, death is relatively far away. As the latter example suggests, words can even carry aspects of things that are not objectively true and have never before been directly experienced. Additionally, words often carry aspects of experiences long past. For example, while driving home from work, you may ruminate about how somebody insulted you during the day, and as a result constantly bring forth the aversive aspects of a past experience simply because these aversive aspects are carried by the words that describe it. This bidirectional characteristic of language essentially helps to ensure that any negatively valenced thought we have carries some of the functions of the experiences those words refer to, even if the words are not actually true, refer to an experience that has come and gone, or refer to a future experience that may never be.

This discussion leads us to one of the defining characteristics of RFT. The act of relating stimuli (e.g., relating the word "milk" to actual milk) leads to the *transformation of stimulus functions*. When two stimuli are related, some of the functions of each stimulus change according to what stimulus it is related to and how it is related to that stimulus. When you first saw the written word "milk" as a small child, it appeared simply as a meaningless set of marks on paper. Once you learned what the word meant, however, it came to carry some of the stimulus functions of actual milk because it is now *framed relationally* with actual milk. In other words, the written word "milk" subsequently came to elicit similar reactions from you that actual milk might; in a psychological sense, you might "see" a glass of milk, feel its coldness, almost taste it and experience its texture, and so on. As another example, imagine you had no negative feelings toward a co-worker named "John." If someone you trust now tells you that "John is a cancer in this organization," you may start to feel negatively toward him because John has been framed as equivalent to the malignant, destructive features of cancer.

Principle 2: Language Processes are Dominant

An astronomical number of verbal relations can be verbally extrapolated (or *derived*) from limited direct experiences. For example, if you are told only that Jim is older than Sam and Sam is older than Bill, you can instantly derive that Jim is older than Bill (*combinatorial entailment*, or CE), Bill is younger than Jim (CE), Sam is younger than Jim (*mutual entailment*, or ME), and Bill is younger than Sam (ME). You were directly taught only two relations, yet were able to derive four more. Unfortunately, such derivations are often not based on objective fact, allowing language to bind us with increasingly subjective bonds. Imagine yourself as a child being told that mistakes are bad, and later making a mistake. "I" is now related to "mistake," which has been previously related to "bad." The *combinatorally entailed* relation between "I" and "bad" would lead you to believe that *you are bad*, even though no one has ever told you that. This relational process may appear simple to the point of being simplistic, yet dozens of carefully controlled RFT experiments have repeatedly shown that language functions precisely in this way. We are relating stimuli constantly, and in an astounding variety of ways (e.g., using hierarchical, spatial, temporal, causal, and comparative relations, as well as relations of equivalence or similarity, and opposition),[6] and each derivation leads to corresponding transformations of stimulus functions.

Research on RFT has indicated that if people are taught just a few relations via direct experience, they can derive an exponential number of relations indirectly, such that a number (x) of directly trained relations will yield a total of x^2 derivations under ideal conditions (e.g., directly training five relations between six stimuli will yield a total of 25 derivations). Thus, the percentage of our understanding that is concretely based on direct experience appears to be quite small compared to the percentage that is derived. Research on RFT also suggests that when our verbal constructions are inconsistent with our experience, the verbal constructions tend strongly to dominate.[1,7] This means that we often trust our thoughts over our own experience, even when it is harmful and/or inaccurate to do so.

Principle 3: Language Greatly Expands Potential Targets of Avoidance

Non-human animals (which existing empirical research strongly suggests are nonverbal according to the RFT definition of language)[7] have a strong tendency to avoid aversive external stimuli. For example, a rat shocked consistently when entering a particular corner of a cage will subsequently avoid that corner. A cat repeatedly harassed by a small child will subsequently avoid that child. Animals do not attempt to avoid words (except in cases where a word like "No" is repeatedly and directly paired with punishment), and do not engage in attempts to avoid aversive emotions in the presence of external stimulation that has been established as threatening or punishing (though we may often anthropomorphize them and assume that they experience and react to emotions as complexly as we do). Human beings, however, actively engage in avoidance of unpleasant thoughts and emotions,[1] often with great frequency. Relational Frame Theory explains that thoughts and emotions become targets of avoidance precisely because words carry stimulus functions of aversive external events.

In and of themselves, thoughts and emotions are not dangerous. No one has ever literally been killed by words (though they might lead someone to "pull the trigger"), and feelings do not appear to result in death either (except, perhaps, in rare cases when heightened anxiety triggers a heart attack in someone physiologically compromised). Thoughts become aversive when verbal learning processes (i.e., mutual and combinatorial entailment) lead them to carry aversive stimulus functions of real or imagined aversive events. Emotions (when divorced from imminent, real physical threat and current aversive stimulation from external sources) become aversive when they are verbally framed in relation to aversive consequences. For example, a feeling of sadness, in and of itself, is not intrinsically harmful. It is perceived as harmful when (for example) it is seen as an indicator of personal deficiency, as a feeling that will never end, as a sign of unfairness, as a sign that there is something wrong with the world, and so on. In other words, sadness and other emotions become harmful because they are framed relationally with more tangibly threatening states of affairs, whether real or imagined.

Once thoughts and emotions are verbally set up as "concrete things" with verbally established aversive qualities, they can become objects of avoidance, thus greatly expanding the range of "things" human beings can now attempt to avoid. Sometimes, such efforts at cognitive and emotional avoidance (termed inclusively as *experiential avoidance*) can be relatively benign and simply involve attempts to (for example) distract oneself from unpleasant thoughts or feelings, mild procrastination, or talking to a friend to try and "make oneself feel better." At other times, experiential avoidance strategies can be quite harmful, as when they involve things like alcohol or substance abuse, extreme isolation, aggression, severe procrastination, and pervasive failures to attend to unpleasant problems which need to be addressed.

Unfortunately, experiential avoidance does not appear to work well in the long run. Research has shown that when subjects are asked to suppress a thought, they later show an increase in this suppressed thought as compared with those not given suppression instructions.[8] Indeed, the suppression strategy may actually stimulate the suppressed mood in a kind of self-amplifying loop.[9,10] Thought suppression has been found to be associated with heightened pain experience,[11] anxiety,[12] poorer ratings of quality of sleep and longer estimates of sleep-onset latency when thoughts are suppressed during the pre-sleep period,[13] and increases in the reinforcing effect of alcohol when urges to drink were suppressed by heavy drinkers.[14] Similar results have been found in the coping literature.[15-17] More broadly, a heightened level of experiential avoidance is correlated with increased anxiety, depression, substance abuse, worry, long-term disability, high-risk sexual behavior, inability to learn, poorer work performance, lower quality of life, and higher degrees of overall psychopathology.[18]

Principle 4: Language Processes are Controlled by Context

Research on RFT indicates that the reason we constantly derive relations, or engage in relational framing, is because the verbal community reinforces such relating. As a simple example, a child may be taught to connect the letters "C" "A" "T" with a picture of a cat and with the sound "CAT." Later, when a cat actually walks by, a parent may ask the child questions like, "What is that?" Without ever being taught the link between the sound and the actual cat, the child may correctly respond "CAT." The parent might then reinforce the child by saying "good!"

Speaking more broadly, there are numerous contexts in which relational framing is reinforced. For example, in the context or "reason giving," the social community reinforces people for providing reasons for their behaviour.[1] If you ask a person with social anxiety, "why didn't you give the speech?," they might respond, "I don't know." Many people would actively discourage this response. If the person said, "I couldn't give the speech because I was anxious," the community would be more likely to find this acceptable. Thus, the person was reinforced for creating a causal "frame" between anxiety and not engaging in a particular behaviour.[5] After many years of such conditioning, self-reinforcement works to maintain relational responding, as when consequences like understanding the reasons for events occurring around us or viewing experiences from a coherent perspective become "intrinsically" reinforcing.[5]

There is now strong evidence that verbal relating is controlled by reinforcement and other contextual conditions, as suggested by RFT.[1,5] In fact, the trio of processes which comprise language from an RFT perspective (mutual entailment, combinatorial entailment, and the transformations of function which arise from these entailments) are theorized to be active *only when certain contextual conditions are in place*. Reinforcement for relating in general and for specific types of relating (e.g., causal relating where thoughts and feelings are established as causes for subsequent behavior) that must be delivered at least intermittently is, of course, one of these contextual conditions, but conventions surrounding the meaningful use of language are critically important as well. For a person to use language with full understanding, basic grammatical conventions must be observed, rate of speech must occur within certain parameters (i.e., such that words are not spoken too quickly or too slowly), the person must have sufficient command of the language (e.g., English, French, German) being used, and the person must attend consistently to the content of what is being thought or spoken in order not to "lose sight" of what is being said. During times when such conditions are violated, RFT predicts that verbal transformations of function will be disrupted – and language will, at least to a degree, temporarily lose its ability to transform experience.

Since relational responding (and the verbal transformations of function which arise from relational responding) is contextually controlled, *and* responsible for thoughts and emotions becoming targets of experiential avoidance, it follows that experiential avoidance is itself contextually controlled. From the perspective of an applied psychologist, this is a very fortunate thing indeed. If language's ability to enhance psychological suffering and increase problematic experiential avoidance is controlled by directly manipulable contextual conditions like reinforcement, standardized grammar and rate of speech, and attention to content, then it follows that *changing these contextual conditions at strategic times should temporarily disrupt language's ability to enhance suffering and increase experiential avoidance*. The majority of this chapter will describe an applied EI training technology intended precisely to accomplish these goals.

Evidence for Mindfulness-Based Emotional Intelligence Training

Acceptance and Commitment Therapy (ACT)[1] was developed to undermine the harmful effects of language described by RFT. We view MBEIT as a type of ACT intervention applied to "non-clinical" populations in group format. The term "MBEIT" is used instead of ACT to avoid some of the pejorative or counterproductive connotations of using words like "acceptance" and "therapy" with normal populations. By focusing on words like "emotionally intelligent behavior," we emphasize to our intervention participants that MBEIT is about promoting effective action in the presence of emotions, rather than about "fixing" emotional "problems."

There is increasing applied evidence that ACT is an effective form of treatment for anxiety, depression, and other clinical disorders.[19] Importantly, more recent studies are suggesting that ACT may be beneficial to "normal" populations, as would be suggested by RFT. Acceptance and Commitment Therapy has been shown to significantly reduce stress and improve health in an organization, compared to a control group, and another intervention program.[20] It was also shown to increase the tendency to engage in organizational innovation.[20] In another study, ACT significantly reduced burnout amongst counselors, when compared to a control group, and another intervention group.[18] It has been shown to reduce speech anxiety and increase the time people were willing to spend making a speech,[21] and it has been shown to increase adherence to difficult self-management regimes in the service of controlling diabetes.[22] Finally, ACT has been shown to dramatically reduce, for example, "bottom line" behaviors such as sick leave utilization amongst chronic pain patients.[23]

☐ Increasing Emotionally Intelligent Behavior

If language is such a problem, then how can the language in this chapter be used to help escape that problem? MBEIT follows a number of rules of thumb to minimize the harmful effects of language. First, MBEIT encourages people to use personal experience as a guide, rather than the words they say or the words we say in a training session. Second, MBEIT emphasizes the use of metaphors (we present visual metaphors below), because metaphors are assumed to facilitate more flexible and less literal understanding than more prescriptive verbal formulations, thus allowing people to contact their personal experience in a potentially more direct and concrete manner.

Third, MBEIT does not engage in thought challenging, confidence building, positive thinking, or any of the techniques commonly seen in cognitive behavioral therapy.[24–26] These techniques tend to be highly analytical, and thus inconsistent with MBEIT's intent to strategically "short-circuit" the problematic aspects of human rationality and logic.[27] MBEIT seeks to help people "step outside" of language for a moment, and to mindfully watch the "languaging mind" as it silently structures the world. We now discuss one way of sequencing and delivering the intervention dimensions of MBEIT. The discussion is purposefully kept in common sense language (i.e., "intervention-speak") rather than technically precise language (i.e., "science-speak") to allow a clearer picture of how it is actually delivered. We should note that the intervention does not have to be run in this order. Table 4.1 presents a summary of all the intervention dimensions. We should also note that we provide only a small sample of methods and often there are many exercises in between the exercises we present in this chapter.

Dimension 1 – Effective Emotional Orientation: Learning to Let Go of the Rope

Our words make monsters seem present. Just thinking about a traumatic event can bring forth anxiety, sweating, and heart palpitations. It is natural to want to avoid these "traumatic" words, just as one would avoid unpleasant things in the external world. However, as we discussed above, avoidance often makes things worse. Its kind of like engaging in a tug of war with a monster. The harder you pull, the harder the monster

TABLE 4.1. Dimensions targeted by Mindfulness-Based Emotional Intelligence Training (MBEIT) that are hypothesized to promote emotionally intelligent behavior

Dimensions	Description
1. Effective emotional orientation	• Willingness to have emotionally charged private experiences (thoughts, images, emotions) when doing so fosters effective action • Accepting the inevitability of a certain amount of unpleasant emotion and negative self-evaluation
2. Defusing from unhelpful rules, evaluations, and other symbolic experience	• Looking at emotionally charged thoughts, rather than through them. Seeing them for what they are (fleeting thoughts that come and go) and not what they seem to be ("realities," facts that must guide behavior, dangers that must be avoided) • Seeing that emotionally charged thoughts about life are not equivalent to life • Being able to be mindful of moment to moment experience (either internal or external) • Escaping the perceived need to defend self-esteem • Recognizing that emotionally charged evaluations of the self do not have to stop us from pursing our goals
3. Being aware of emotions	• Being able to identify emotions in self and others • Noticing the evaluations and thoughts that often occur with emotions • Noticing how emotions progress over time, how they come and go • Noticing details of the situation associated with emotions
4. Effective action orientation	• Ability to take action that is consistent with goals and values, in the context of: impulses, fears, lack of confidence, low emotional awareness, uncertainty, exhaustion, fatigue, physical pain, intense emotion • Awareness of own values • Ability to sustain committed action in the face of inconsistent feedback, frustration, and failure

pulls. You never seem to gain ground, and meanwhile life is passing you by (Figure 4.1).

MBEIT does not seek to persuade people of this point. "Persuading" would just be another form of getting people to believe words. Instead, MBEIT helps people to contact their experience with avoidance strategies. It helps them to notice whether or not the strategy is working. Through experiencing some avoidance strategies as unworkable, they learn an alternative to avoidance – acceptance, or willingness to experience unpleasant thoughts and feelings. Essentially, they learn that they can let go of the rope (Figure 4.2).

FIGURE 4.1 Struggling to get rid of our emotions can be like playing tug of war with a monster.

FIGURE 4.2 Sometimes the best thing to do is let go of the rope.

Exercise 1: Discovering the Pervasiveness of Avoidance

The first step in helping people to learn acceptance is to help them to identify the variety of ways in which they avoid. We normally get people to list avoidance strategies and write them on a board. People come to realize just how pervasive avoidance is in our culture. They realize that they avoid unpleasant emotions by drinking, watching TV, procrastinating, trying to think positive thoughts, distracting themselves, avoiding negative thoughts, and so on. People also realize that they engage in many behaviors that are designed to avoid interpersonal discomfort. For example, to avoid "feeling small," they may "play big." To avoid feelings of fear, embarrassment, or anger that occur due to inter-personal conflict, they may avoid asserting themselves, or they may attempt to "get rid of the conflict" by behaving aggressively.[28] To avoid feeling guilty, parents may avoid punishing their children and be too permissive. Or to avoid feeling embarrassed by bad behavior in public, parents may engage in excessively harsh punishment.[29] Though all these behaviors appear quite different, they are all presumed to serve the same function – namely, to reduce unpleasant affect.

After people have made a comprehensive list of avoidance strategies (and contrasted these "emotion-focused" strategies to generated "active coping" strategies intended toward constructive action and not experien-tial avoidance), we ask them to contact, in their own experiences, the extent to which these strategies work for them. It is not our goal to convince people that avoidance does not work. Rather, the goal is to help them notice when avoidance does and does not work for them. Often people will start to realize that many of the strategies they use do not work in the long run. They may feel upset that they have been wasting so much time trying to escape the inescapable. However, they also often feel a sense of relief once they notice that these strategies, uniformly, are not working for others in the room as well. They begin to notice it is not "just them" who fail to banish unwanted feelings, especially when it matters most. They begin to notice that perhaps there is something more universal about the ineffectiveness of experiential avoidance. This sets the stage for techniques like the next one, which begin to explain why (in metaphorical and experiential terms) such avoidance attempts often fail.

Exercise 2: The Lie Detector[1]

Imagine that you are hooked up to a lie detector, which is able to detect any increase in anxiety. Your task is to not feel anxious for the next five minutes. Of course there is always a chance that you will not be sufficiently motivated to do the task. Indeed, is it not common sense that if you cannot get over an unwanted emotion like anxiety, you are just not trying hard enough to resolve it (e.g., people often say "just get over it" or "pull yourself up by your boots")? So, in order to motivate you properly, we will point a gun to your head, and if you still cannot eliminate the anxiety, we will pull the trigger.

People quickly realize that they would be unable to control their anx-iety in this situation. We then contrast it with another situation. Let us say I pointed a gun to your head and told you that you have five minutes to get me a glass of water. You may feel terrified, but you would probably be able to get the water. This exercise allows us to introduce the possibility that there are two rules in operation here.

1. *The rule of public experience:* If you are not willing to have it, you are usually able to get rid of it. For example, you can always get rid of an ugly sofa, clean a dirty house, or drive to the store and buy groceries. Often, if you do not like something going on in the world "outside the skin," you can simply identify what the problem is, and change it.
2. *The rule of private experience:* If you are not willing to have it, you have it – sometimes even more of it. If you try to get rid of your anxiety (for example), you will often experience more anxiety, as failures to control the anxiety in important situations typically breed additional anxiety about the ineffectiveness of your attempts and the imagined consequences of feeling anxious.

Dimension 2 – Defusing Language: Learning to See the Prison Bars for What they Are, Not What they Say they Are

Cognitive fusion refers to the process by which verbal formulations (evaluations and rules) take on the apparent ability to control subsequent behavior. For example, someone might evaluate their anxiety as "horrible." The "horrible" evaluation may make "anxiety" feel more aversive (see language section above), and may make it more likely for someone to engage in avoidance of the anxiety. Additionally, a variety of rules about how one "must" or "should" behave, and about how emotions and thoughts prohibit some actions and necessitate others, are often generated. For example, a stereotypical male might hold to the notion that he "cannot show emotion," as a stereotypical female might believe that acting assertively or confrontationally is an impossibility.

Another broad class of verbal rules casts thoughts and emotions as inevitable causes for subsequent behavior. For example, one might assume that calm and consistent parenting is only possible when anger or frustration is not being felt, or that one can act in a loving manner toward one's spouse only when loving *feelings* are present. Conversely, one might believe that strong anger must inevitably lead to an argument, or high anxiety to disengagement from the anxiety-provoking task. These rules, when believed, prompt people to engage in unhelpful emotional control strategies (see previous dimension) or lead them to stop engaging in valued actions.

Defusion does not involve changing the form or frequency of aversive thoughts. Rather, defusion strategies aim to demonstrate that apparently problematic verbal rules and evaluations are not as solid and binding as

FIGURE 4.3 When rules and evaluations are literally believed, they can act as prison bars.

they appear to be. Rather than providing clients with advice about how to "get rid of" troublesome or "counter-productive" thoughts, defusion strategies work to change the client's relation to these thoughts and expose them simply as words rather than binding realities.

Defusion involves learning to see the bars for what they are (streams of thoughts, fleeting sensations) and not what they say they are (iron barriers). From a human perspective, such rules and evaluations often seem as solid and prohibitive as the bars they are written on (Figure 4.3). However, from the view of a nonverbal organism, the evaluations and rules are meaningless sounds, not actual physical barriers. Defusion strategies attempt to create a context where clients experience these "prison bars" in a way that is significantly closer to how the dog in Figure 4.4 experiences them. In other words, defusion strategies work to get clients to experience language – especially their own debilitating negative self-evaluations and counterproductive behavioral rules – in ways that highlight language's unique ability to create prisons that are not really there.

FIGURE 4.4 Here is how a nonverbal creature views your prison.

Exercise 1: Finding the Descriptions, Evaluations, and Rules

From an MBEIT or ACT perspective, language is useful when it allows us to describe events and experiences, and to evaluate and plan in ways that allow increasingly effective action. However, language can be harmful when the negative evaluations and overly prescriptive rules it generates cause unnecessary suffering and self-sabotaging behavior. This exercise is designed to help people experience the difference between descriptions on the one hand, and potentially problematic rules and evaluations on the other hand.

Like all exercises in MBEIT, the goal is not to argue about the truth or falseness of particular thoughts or evaluations. Rather, the goal is to identify evaluations and thoughts that are acting as barriers to effective action, and to change the context in which they occur so that they are no longer barriers.

Throughout this exercise, people should be encouraged to *experience* the difference between descriptions, evaluations, and rules, rather than to *understand* this difference via reasoning. We also want to encourage people to look *at* their private experiences, rather than *through* them. Using categories like "descriptions," "evaluations," and "rules" helps people to observe their private experiences, rather than getting caught up in them.

It should be mentioned that this exercise is more extensive than written, with frequent requests to check with one's immediate experience and see if there appears to be a "gut-level" difference between the concrete, tangible aspects of a description and the abstract referents of evaluations and abstract rules. The purpose of the exercise is to give the client direct experiential contact with the relative "emptiness" of abstract evaluations and abstract rules. In contrast to descriptions, which refer directly to formal stimulus properties (i.e., characteristics that can be directly perceived with one of the five senses), evaluations have no physical referents, yet people typically react to their own evaluations as if they were as immutably solid as descriptions. When clients experience for themselves that there are no clear referents for evaluations (that they do not refer to any tangible qualities), they tend to take these evaluations less seriously. At no point during the exercise should the trainer try to talk the client into believing that there is a difference between descriptions and evaluations, or convince the client that descriptions are "true" and evaluations are "false." Rather, the trainer should explicitly remind the client that she is not trying to make a logical point and is not trying to convince the client of anything. The client should be repeatedly asked to check in with his own experience to see if these distinctions resonate "at a gut level," and the trainer should trust that a properly structured exercise will allow the client to make this experiential realization.

Descriptions are thoughts that simply describe the directly observable aspects of things. For example:

- *This is a table* (tables are hard, solid, have four or more legs, etc.)
- *I am feeling anxiety* (anxiety consists of certain physical sensations and urges)
- *My friend is yelling at me* (he/she is speaking loudly and quickly at me, gesturing wildly)

Evaluations are thoughts that compare events and assign an evaluative label (like good or bad, unbearable or bearable, rude or polite, prohibitive or permissive, shameful, embarrassing, and any other way of negatively or positively evaluating feelings, events, people, or experiences). For example:

- This is a *good* table
- This anxiety is *unbearable* (or bad, or prevents me from giving this speech, etc.)
- My friend is a *jerk* for yelling at me (or I cannot handle being yelled at, or I need to yell back at him to prove my point, etc.)

Rules refer to explicit or implicit ideas about how things have to be done, or cannot be done. The kinds of rules targeted by MBEIT trainers are similar to evaluations in that these rules do not refer to tangible, directly sense-able *descriptive* statements like "I can't walk on water," or "Don't walk in front of a moving car or you'll get hurt." Rather, they refer to abstract ideas about what one should and should not do, unnecessarily rigid ways of problem-solving, or culturally prevalent or idiosyncratic rules about how thoughts and emotions relate to subsequent behavior. Some examples include: rules about emotions (e.g., "Men don't cry; women don't get angry"; "If I get anxious, I will just lose control"; "No pain, no gain") and rules about how people and life should not make us upset (e.g., "People must treat me fairly; The world must be fair"; "I must always perform well at everything I do"; "Don't trust . . . (type of cultural group, religious group, individuals with certain occupations)").

Thus, *descriptions* are solid. *Evaluations and rules* are a bit fishier and less substantial than descriptions. To keep things simple, the next part of the exercise focuses on the distinction between descriptions and evaluations. Rules are dealt with at various points throughout the intervention.

We often believe that our evaluative opinions are just as solid as descriptions, yet when we examine evaluations more closely they start to look a little fishy. Evaluations of these events differ depending on cultural or personal opinion, so descriptions describe events or experiences that are "firm to the touch" and evaluations and rules are not as solid. We do not have to treat evaluations as if they are "true" with a capital "T." We can choose to leave them alone if they help us achieve our goals and put our values into play, or we can choose to notice them and not believe them if they hold us back.

At this point, the facilitator completes a couple of examples to help the participants see, at a gut level, the difference between descriptions and evaluations. We draw a line down the middle of a whiteboard, and write down a fairly comprehensive list of descriptions and evaluations for different emotions. For example, we may consider anxiety. Descriptions typically include statements like "tight stomach," "slight pain in shoulders," "thoughts about failing," and "faster breathing." Evaluations typically include statements like "Anxiety is bad" and "Anxiety means you are weak." Clients may have difficulty coming up with evaluative and rule-related statements about anxiety initially, so they are often prompted with statements like "What does it say about you as a person when you feel really, really anxious?," or "If you're really anxious, how does this affect what you do next?"

After completing a couple of examples on the whiteboard, we then present a metaphor. We ask participants to consider looking at descriptions and evaluations in a different way, and then put up the stars slide (Figure 4.5).

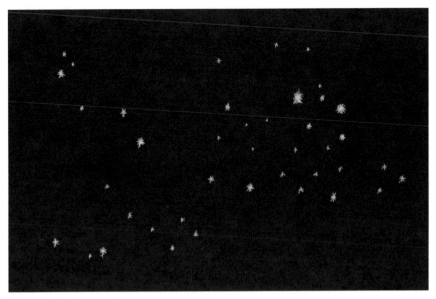

FIGURE 4.5 Stars in the sky.

We ask them to look at the slide and describe what they see. Participants generally describe the physical attributes of the shapes on the slide and the colour of the shapes. We then indicate that this slide represents the constellation of Leo (the lion).

The facilitator then shows the slide of the lion (Figure 4.6), as it would be if mapped onto the stars. The participants are asked to look again at the slide of the stars and then are asked the following: "Do you see the lion in this slide? If you look at this constellation in the sky, do you see a lion? One of the big errors we make as human beings is mistaking evaluations for descriptions. Descriptions are solid, like these stars – like this table. We could actually map on each of these descriptors for anxiety to each of these stars. Do these descriptions of anxiety feel as solid as these stars? And then our minds start getting creative, spitting out all these evaluations that turn this (point to stars) into something scary like this (point to three-dimensional lion). But is the lion really there? Are these evaluations really solid? Can they really hurt us? Can this lion up in the sky really hurt you?"

As can be seen by the sample dialogue above, the facilitator systematically "maps on" the description–evaluation distinction to the star–lion distinction. Discuss with participants that actual anxiety does not seem to be so scary at the descriptive level, but the evaluations are even scarier. Perhaps there is a possibility that the struggle that we humans go through may be a result of us taking the evaluations as seriously as the

FIGURE 4.6 The constellation Leo. Our interpretation of the stars.

descriptions, as though the evaluations are as solid as the descriptions. Typically, clients resonate with the example, because they recall seeing fanciful three-dimensional renderings of zodiacal constellations as school children. They quickly latch on to the comparison between evaluations and the "3D lion." Whereas the stars and descriptions that underlay these constructions are solid and directly sense-able, the evaluations and 3D lion "are not really solid."

Exercise 2: Say it Funny, Say it Slow, and Say it Till you Can Say it No More

As illustrated by the "description–evaluation" exercise, language must be used in certain ways in order to fully change one's experience. When the discrepancy between evaluative language and direct experience is fully recognized, for example, these words lose much of their power over our behaviour. Another way to disrupt this context of "normal" language use can involve speaking problematic evaluations or rules at an unusually slow rate or in a funny voice. Try saying "I'm not good enough" extremely slowly (e.g., one syllable on an in-breath, the next on an out-breath, and so on). Now try saying it in the funniest voice you can think of, or even singing the words as part of a familiar melody. You may likely find that you experience these words a bit differently, that they lose some of their power over you.

Words must be spoken at a certain speed (not too fast, not too slow) in order to be fully meaningful, and troublesome negative evaluations are virtually always spoken or thought of in a serious tone of voice. Violating these normalities changes "what shows up" when such words are considered. Another exercise involves repeating a short, problematic verbal phrase again and again. Try repeating "I'm ugly," "I'm bad," or "I'm fat" (or some other short, self-pejorative phrase) fifty to sixty times, fairly quickly. If you are unwilling to try this with negatively self-evaluative words, simply try repeating the word "milk" over and over. What happens to the words? Whereas these words initially focused on the aversive content they referred to, by the end of the exercise only the sound of the words and the sensation of speaking them remained.

When language is used meaningfully, words are not repeated to such an extreme extent. When they are, they lose the power to bring their abstract referents into the room. The point of these exercises is not to challenge or refute verbal content. It is essentially to expose the illusory quality of language, to temporarily disrupt language's ability to create evaluative or prescriptive fictions. Ultimately, from an ACT/MBEIT perspective, the purpose of such defusion exercises is to help the client experience problematic evaluations and rules simply as words, not as concrete barriers to effective value-driven action.

Exercise 3: Learning to Look At Thoughts, Rather than Through Them

People typically assume that their interpretations of experiences perfectly describe these experiences. In other words, when we evaluate our experience or confine our behavior according to arbitrary verbal rules, we assume that these evaluations and rules are binding realities, especially when there is strong emotion attached to these thoughts. We do not consider the possibility that these evaluations and rules are perhaps *just words*, and that our actual direct experience and behavioral options may deviate markedly from these words. To further help clients look more clearly *at* their thoughts and the contexts they occur in, we often have them complete the ABC Worksheet (see Appendix A).

The ABC exercise helps clients to break their experience up into its parts. It helps them to notice the difference between descriptions of the situation, and the evaluations and rules they lay on top of these descriptions. It also helps them to notice the distinction between believing thoughts and not believing thoughts. Finally, it helps focus more clearly on the potentially value-inconsistent consequences of "buying into" problematic evaluations and rules.

Exercise 4: Becoming Mindful of Private Experiences (Thoughts, Images, Sounds, Sensations)

A big part of almost every exercise in MBEIT involves helping people to look *at* their private experiences ("defusing"), rather than *through* them. The intent is to change the context in which these private experiences occur, rather than changing their actual content. Mindfulness exercises can be quite effective at changing people's perspective on private experience, as they involve noticing what private experiences show up and accepting those experiences as they come and go, rather than trying to change or modify them. This is a shift from "doing" something about thoughts and feelings, to just "being with" thoughts and feelings. It is also a shift from being "lost in one's words," to being present with one's moment to moment experience, while words keep flowing like a stream alongside you.

There are a substantial number of mindfulness exercises that can be used.[1,30–32] We have found in our workshops that people differ in their ability to practice mindfulness meditations. Thus, we use a very simple mindfulness practice, taken from Zen Buddhism.[33] While a condensed version of the exercise follows, it should be made clear that his exercise should not simply be read. There should, for example, be many pauses, and the instructions should be given gradually over an extended period of time. After completing the exercise, people are asked about their experience during it. Trainers should ask questions at this point that help to put clients in touch with how often their attention veered away from their breath and got lost in a stream of thoughts, how their experiences differed when they were focused on the moment rather than carried away by their minds, and what it was like to have thoughts and feelings and not do anything about them.

Mindfulness of the breath   Please get comfortable in your chair and close your eyes. Now, follow the sensation of your breath as it flows in through the nostrils and fills the chest and abdomen. Try maintaining attention on the diaphragm or at the nostrils. Just notice your breath as it enters and exits your body.

If you notice yourself being distracted from the breath, that is ok. You cannot possibly do this exercise incorrectly. Just gently bring yourself back to the breath every time you notice your attention has veered away from it. Each time your mind wanders, practice patiently bringing it back to the breath.

Now, I would like you to count each inhalation. Each time you inhale count 1, 2, 3 until you get to 10. Then start at 1 again.

You will notice that thoughts and maybe worries show up. Just notice these thoughts and gently bring yourself back to the breath. You may notice a feeling or sensation. Just notice it and bring yourself back to counting the breath.

There is no need to get rid of these thoughts or feelings. You can just be present with them. Do not try to do anything about them. See if you can just let yourself have them when they show up . . . acknowledge their presence . . . let them be there . . . and then gently focus your attention back on your breath.

You may notice that you have stopped counting and been caught up in a line of thought. Whenever you notice that this has happened, gently bring yourself back to your breath, as many times as it takes.

Notice how your mind wanders and how very difficult it is to control your thoughts.

Exercise 5: Facilitating an Observer Perspective

Nearly all defusion techniques at least implicitly encourage the client to *observe* thoughts and feelings as they occur. However, it is useful to help clients experience this *observer perspective* more explicitly, as a constant perspective from which they can view unpleasant thoughts and emotions as something different from self-defining events. Typically, we assume that our recurring thoughts and emotions define us, that we are the sum total of what we think and feel. Experiencing a sense of *self as observer*, rather than *self as the content of one's thoughts and feelings*, helps clients more consistently experience potentially problematic thoughts and feelings as richly verbal events, not self-defining realities. The *observer* is the one constant across all one's experiences. While thoughts, feelings, sensations, and roles change, one always has the ability to "step behind" these experiences and watch them come and go. To paraphrase Jon Kabat-Zinn, "wherever *you* go [and whatever *you* say or do], there *you* are."[31] This "observer self" has also been described as a sense of *self as context* – that is, one's self as a context or arena in which various types of psychological content such as thoughts and feelings unfold (Figure 4.7) – versus a sense of *self as content*, where one's self is defined according to the content of what is psychologically experienced.[1]

There are a number of exercises that are designed to put people in touch with this observer self, at an experiential level.[1] Underlying all these exercises is an intent to help people find a safe place from which they can observe all their passing emotions and evaluations. Once people experience the observer self across a variety of situations, they are generally in a better position to notice and un-hook from problematic evaluations and rules.

Even evaluations and rules with apparently "positive" content can impede effective movement toward one's values if fused with. For

FIGURE 4.7 The self-as-context.

instance, if a client holds tightly to thoughts like "I'm special," "I'm highly respected," or "I'm a very important person" (or believes that he *must* have such experiences constantly), he might focus much of his behavior on creating or maintaining such circumstances *even if such behavior does not move him closer to what he finds truly meaningful in his life*. In such situations, it may often be helpful to ask clients questions like, "If you buy into this thought, does it take you in a direction that you *truly* value going?" (Figure 4.8a,b,c).

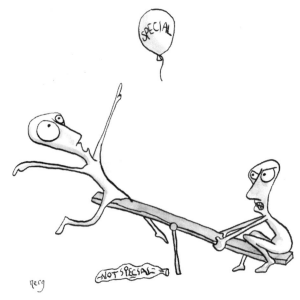

FIGURE 4.8a Struggling to feel special can hurt your relationships. As you struggle to be more special, you may make others feel less special.

FIGURE 4.8b The struggle is an illusion. A nonverbal animal (e.g., a dog) would not be able to see the "special" evaluation, or smell it, or taste it. The dog would not know what all the fuss is about.

FIGURE 4.8c What positive evaluation do you pursue (e.g., "special," "strong," "admirable," "perfect," "attractive")? Write it in the balloons.

Dimension 3 – Emotional Awareness

This dimension involves the ability to identify emotions in the self and others, to notice the evaluations and thoughts that show up with different emotions, and to notice how emotions progress over time. In MBEIT, the interventions designed to improve emotional awareness are done indirectly, by increasing acceptance and mindfulness/defusion (i.e., the first three dimensions in Table 4.1). Research has found that people who chronically tend to accept experiences and be mindful of them also tend to be the best at identifying their feelings.[34,35]

It is important to note that at no point in an MBEIT intervention do we encourage people to reason about the causes and consequences of emotions. The hypothesis is that reinforcing reasoning will also reinforce people's belief that "reasons" can stop them from taking valued action (e.g., "I can't do this, because I am too anxious."). While it is often valuable for clients to notice the contexts in which they tend to feel certain ways (as this may often facilitate their readiness to defuse, accept, and move toward personally held values), placing primary emphasis on exactly "why" one feels what one feels can tend to reaffirm the illusion that thoughts and feelings dictate action. Instead, we use more non-analytic, mindfulness techniques to help people to accept and become aware of their emotions (e.g., see the Tin-Can Monster exercise below). Our goal is to help people to notice their emotion-relevant sensations and thoughts, and then notice whether believing these thoughts will help them move toward what they value. For example, people who experience anger often think that somebody did something wrong to them. Once people notice they are having thoughts about right or wrong, they can choose to believe them – for example, by seeking to make things fair again, or seeking to condemn or retaliate against the wrongdoing. Or, they can choose to just notice the "right" and "wrong" evaluations and not believe them, if believing them would move them further away from what they value (e.g., as when "being right" means destroying a valued relationship).

Accepting emotions and being mindfully aware of them is expected to have another benefit. It is hypothesized to increase awareness of all the details of the situation associated with the previously avoided emotions. For example, if someone is not willing to feel anger, they are often not willing to focus on situational details that elicit that anger. They may need to focus on these details if they are to problem solve and move toward values in a maximally effective manner. Consistent with this view, research suggests that people who have trouble identifying their feelings also have trouble engaging in effective problem solving,[36] turning instead to ineffective avoidance strategies such as alcohol and drug use.[37]

Exercise 1: The Tin-Can Monster: Strengthening your Awareness and Willingness Skills

It is one thing to realize that avoidance often does not work, and another thing altogether to actually stop avoiding. An MBEIT intervention is designed to help people become aware of potentially unhelpful feelings and thoughts, and to give people experience at engaging in willingness/acceptance moves in relation to those feelings and thoughts.

The tin-can monster exercise seeks to give people practice giving up the struggle with emotional discomfort and disturbing thoughts. It is also designed to help them experience the natural ebb and flow of willingness, to realize that it is not something that they will "get" and "have" forever. The exercise instructions go something like this:

> Willingness can often be like facing a giant, 30 foot monster who is made up of tin cans and strings. It is almost impossible to face this monster willingly. However, if we disassemble him into all the cans, string, and wire that he's made of, each of those individual pieces is easier to face up to. . . .

Now, if you are willing, get comfortable and relaxed, shut your eyes, and think of a specific feeling or situation. The situation should be something that you are currently struggling with, something that is important to you. I want you to try to get in touch with the feeling or situation that you've chosen. Notice first if there are any bodily sensations that are associated with what you've chosen. As you think about it, just gently notice what your body is feeling, what your body is doing, and if you notice some specific reaction, just pull it up and look at it. Now, I want you to spend some time letting go of the struggle with that specific bodily feeling. The goal here is not that you like the feeling, but that you are willing to have it and not struggle with it.[1]

Once one sensation has been targeted, the exercise is repeated for other sensations, emotions, and memories associated with the struggle. In the metaphor, each of these private experiences is like some part of the tin-can monster. Together, they can seem overwhelming, yet individually, they are exposed as less dangerous.

The goal of learning willingness and acceptance is not to help people to "wallow" in their emotions. Rather, it is to give people an enhanced ability to pursue their values, as unpleasant emotions and thoughts often occur in the pursuit of values and thus must often be accepted. Thus, we encourage them to choose acceptance when doing so helps them to achieve their values (see next dimension). Every strategy used in MBEIT is ultimately intended to help the client more effectively work toward a more valued way of living.

Dimension 4 – Effective Action Orientation: Learning to Journey in a Direction that you Value and to Stay on your Chosen Path Despite all the Swamps and Distractions

Ultimately, everything in MBEIT is done in the service of helping the client develop a more effective action orientation, which can be defined as the ability to take action consistent with personally held values and goals, even when unpleasant thoughts and emotions are present. This part of the intervention involves helping people to clarify what they value and to make contact with what it takes to stay committed to a valued course of action (Figure 4.9).

Values can be defined as "verbally construed global life consequences".[1] [(p. 206)] More directly, values can be thought of as ways of acting and living that impart meaning and vitality to one's life. The ACT/MBEIT perspective on values thus casts them not as culturally-based prescriptions about what one *should* value, but rather as intensely personal choices that *truly* create personal meaning and vitality.

FIGURE 4.9 A visual metaphor of effective action orientation.

Exercise 1: Attending your Own Funeral

When faced with our own imminent mortality, what is most important to us can often become very clear. The "Funeral exercise"[1] helps clients experientially contact how they would *really* like to be remembered for living their lives – what a life really worth living looks like to each of them. Clients are asked to imagine that they have died and that somehow they can witness their own funeral. They are asked to imagine that everybody important to them is at funeral. What would each of those people say about how the client lived her life? More importantly, what would the client most like to hear these people say about how she lived her life?

We encourage clients to not think in terms of limitations or what is likely. Rather they are encouraged to think of how they would ideally like to be remembered, in a world where they could choose anything. The exercise is excellent for drawing people's attention to values they have stopped living or neglected. An alternative, similar exercise involves having people imagine what epitaph they would like to have put on their tombstone. It is rare for people to say something like "He worked 60 hours a week and managed to reach senior management at Morgan and Stern." Rather, people often make contact with values they have neglected, such as "being a supportive husband" or "being a loving mother."

Exercise 2: Values and Goals and Reasons, Oh My

Having cued people to their values, we help them to connect to the distinction between values and goals. Metaphorically, we describe values as a compass. They show you which direction to head. You never completely get there. Your valued direction guides you the way that the stars sometimes guide a sailor. The stars provide consistent direction, although the sailor never reaches them.

Examples of value statements might include being a loving parent, or having intimate, trusting relationships. In contrast, goals are thought of as involving the completion of discrete behavioral tasks that move one closer toward a given value. If one valued being a loving and supportive parent, for example, concordant goals might include regularly scheduling family activities, becoming involved in your child's education, or regularly expressing your approval and appreciation of your child's good behavior. Setting and achieving goals is one way to tell you are moving toward your values.

There are a couple of important characteristics of values. First, they cannot be cancelled or forfeited by failure to act consistently with them at any given time. Thus, acting like a bad parent on Tuesday does not cancel out the value of "being a good parent;" nor does it prevent one from acting like a good parent on Wednesday. As illustrated by Figure 4.10, valuing often involves failing and recommitting again and again. As clients may often think they have "ruined things" when they "fall off the wagon" by doing something that violates what they value, it is important to emphasize that a value can be moved toward at literally any moment, regardless of what was done in the previous moment.

Second, although values often have "reasons" associated with them, they are never chosen *for* reasons. One cannot justify values with reasons. Rather, values are simply chosen. This distinction is important for two interrelated reasons. First, clients often feel the need to justify their values, with the unfortunate consequence that, if they cannot be justified at any given time, they are not valid. Second, if a client needs reasons to value something, he cannot move toward that value unless those reasons are satisfied. For example, a client might believe that he values being a caring and supportive spouse *because* his wife behaves in this manner toward him. If, at any given time, his wife ceases to behave this way toward him for a while, his apparent reason for being caring and supportive is not there to guide his actions. Values do not depend on something as fleeting as reasons. They depend on courses of action that the client has found, over time, to bring increased meaning and vitality to her life. One can choose to act in a manner consistent with one's values at any time, regardless of what reasons (or other thoughts) or feelings are present.

FIGURE 4.10 Valued action often involves many detours and barriers. They require one to keep on recommitting to the value.

Exercise 3: Value Clarification

During this phase, we use a number of exercises to help clients individually clarify values that are personally important. We go through great pains to ensure that they identify *actual* individual values, not values that are being endorsed simply because that is what they have been taught or because they are complying with what somebody else wants. For example, we might ask clients if they would still hold a particular value if nobody knew they held it.

We then have clients complete a values worksheet that systematically samples different value domains, including relationships, education and personal development, recreation/leisure, health/physical well being, and career/employment.[38] Below we provide sample instructions for the worksheet and for one value domain.

> On this worksheet, it is important that you write down what you would most like to strive for. We are not asking what you think you could realistically get, or what others think you deserve. We want to know what you care about, what you would want to work toward, in the best of all situations. While doing the worksheet, pretend that magic happened and that anything is possible.

1) Friendships. In this section, write down what it means to you to be a good friend. If you were able to be the best friend possible, how would you behave toward your friends? Try to describe an ideal friendship.

Exercise 4: Bringing all the Emotional Intelligence Dimensions Together

Appendix B brings all the MBEIT dimensions together on one worksheet. It begins by directing the client to declare a value. Then, the client is asked to list concrete goals and actions that would put the value into play. The next section asks the client to write down and look at the apparent psychological barriers (i.e., feelings, evaluations, and rules) that might show up during the course of value-driven action. Finally, the worksheet asks the client if she is willing to have these unpleasant thoughts and feelings show up in the course of pursuing that value. Clients are encouraged to use defusion strategies to "cut through" apparent verbal barriers that arise in the course of pursuing such values, and acceptance strategies to "sit with" the difficult emotions and experiences that make themselves present.

☐ Conclusions

One of the distinctive features of ACT/MBEIT is that it is based in a clear philosophical framework (i.e., functional contextualism) and theoretical framework (i.e., RFT). There is a rigorous program of basic laboratory research testing RFT, with now over 50 peer-reviewed empirical publications supporting it.[5,39] In addition, there are substantial peer-reviewed publications supporting the applied benefits of ACT/MBEIT for clinical populations and an increasing number of studies showing its benefits to "normal populations."[40] Thus, we can argue that MBEIT is not just an eclectic slew of techniques thrown haphazardly together because they seem reasonable. The theory underlying MBEIT makes very specific predictions about what sorts of techniques and strategies will work (i.e., those promoting acceptance, defusion, and valued action). It also predicts that certain techniques and strategies (e.g., cognitive restructuring, self-esteem building, positive thinking, some forms of relaxation training) will often be less effective than hoped.[41]

There are some striking differences between MBEIT and other EI programs and models. First, we focus on EIB rather than on underlying dispositions. There is much disagreement about what kind of disposition EI is, specifically regarding whether it is "IQ-like"[42–44] or more similar to a personality trait.[45–47] While this is an important question, a functional contextualism framework does not depend on its resolution in order for relevant basic experimental and applied work to continue. Our primary goals are to predict and influence behavior, or, more specifically, to promote value congruent behavior in the context of emotions and emotionally charged thoughts.

Second, unlike all other EI models, our model does not have a managing emotions dimension.[45,46,48,49] The theory underlying MBEIT suggests that attempts to manage emotions are often the problem, not the solution. In most contexts, it is possible to have strong emotions *and* still act effectively. MBEIT helps people to accept and stay mindfully present with their thoughts and feelings, whilst simultaneously undermining the apparent power of those thoughts and feelings to push people off their valued path.

☐ Appendix A: ABC Worksheet

A = Activating Event

Provide a description of an event you have found difficult or challenging. Describe it "as a camera would see it."

Emotional responses associated with A:
Describe any feelings or sensations you notice as you think about the activating event:

B = Believed Thoughts

What kinds of thoughts show up for you when you think about "A"?
Be uninhibited when you complete this section. Write down any thought, no matter how silly or "irrational" it sounds. Then notice which thoughts really tend to grab you and almost push you into doing something. Underline those thoughts.
You may notice "musts," "shoulds," awfulizing, or a tendency to evaluate yourself

C = Consequences (behavioral)
Likely behavioral outcome if you *"buy"* or really believe the thoughts

Likely behavioral outcome if you have the thoughts, but *don't* buy or believe them

☐ Appendix B: Willingness and Commitment Worksheet

What value do you want to put into (more) play in your life?
Values are like guiding stars. You set your course by them, but you never actually
  reach them, or permanently realize them.

Now pick a goal that you would like to achieve, with respect to the value, that
  would let you know that you are "on track."

Now pick an action(s) that will lead you to accomplish that goal.

What stuff seems to stop you from achieving these goals?

Emotions and sensations?

Unhelpful rules (musts, shoulds) and evaluations (It's awful; I can't stand it; I'm
  not good enough)?

Other stuff?

The key here is to look at this private stuff as what it is (just stuff), not what it says it is.

Private stuff seems more powerful than reality sometimes. It often says it is something that is dangerous, or something that is literally true.
Take anxiety. It says it is powerful, like you have to run away from it or listen to what it says.
Notice how "anxiety" is just a word that describes a bunch of fleeting thoughts and feelings.
Notice how you can have those thoughts and feelings and still do what you value.
Are you willing to make room for the thoughts and feelings that show up as a result of your committed action?

Yes (go forward with your journey and experience it!)

No (go back and choose a different valued action, and repeat this exercise. Or practice the defusion exercises and redo this sheet)

☐ References

1. Hayes, S. C., Strosahl, K. D., & Wilson, K. G. (1999). *Acceptance and commitment therapy: An experiential approach to behavior change*: New York: Guilford Press.
2. American Psychiatric Association (1952). *Diagnostic and statistical manual of mental disorders*. Washington, DC: American Psychiatric Association.
3. American Psychiatric Association (1994). *Diagnostic and statistical manual of mental disorders, fourth edition*. Washington, DC: American Psychiatric Association.
4. Csikszentmihalyi, M. (1999). If we are so rich, why aren't we happy? *American Psychologist, 54*, 821–827.
5. Hayes, S. C., Barnes-Holmes, D., & Roche, B. (2001). *Relational frame theory: A post-Skinnerian account of human language and cognition*. New York: Kluwer Academic/Plenum Publishers.
6. Hayes, S. C., Fox, E., Gifford, E. V., Wilson, K. G., Barnes-Holmes, D., & Healy, O. (2001). Derived relational responding as learned behavior. In S. C. Hayes, D. Barnes-Holmes, & B. Roche (Eds.), *Relational frame theory: A post-Skinnerian account of human language and cognition* (pp. 21–49). New York: Kluwer Academic/Plenum Publishers.
7. Hayes, S. C., Brownstein, A. J., Haas, J. R., & Greenway, D. E. (1986). Instructions, multiple schedules, and extinction: Distinguishing rule-governed from schedule-controlled behavior. *Journal of the Experimental Analysis of Behavior, 46*, 137–147.
8. Wenzlaff, R. M., & Wegner, D. M. (2000). Thought suppression. *Annual Review of Psychology, 51*, 59–91.
9. Feldner, M., Zvolensky, M., Eifert, G., & Spira, A. (2003). Emotional avoidance: An experimental test of individual differences and response suppression using biological challenge. *Behaviour Research and Therapy, 41*, 403–411.
10. Wegner, D. M., Erber, R., & Zanakos, S. (1993). Ironic processes in the mental control

of mood and mood-related thought. *Journal of Personality and Social Psychology, 65,* 1093–1104.

11. Sullivan, M. J. L., Rouse, D., Bishop, S., & Johnston, S. (1997). Thought suppression, catastrophizing, and pain. *Cognitive Therapy and Research, 21,* 555–568.

12. Koster, E. H. W., Rassin, E., Crombez, G., & Naring, G. W. B. (2003). The paradoxical effects of suppressing anxious thoughts during imminent threat. *Behaviour Research and Therapy, 41,* 1113–1120.

13. Harvey, A. G. (2003). The attempted suppression of presleep cognitive activity in insomnia. *Cognitive Therapy and Research, 27,* 593–602.

14. Palfai, T. P., Monti, P. M., Colby, S. M., & Rohsenow, D. J. (1997). Effects of suppressing the urge to drink on the accessibility of alcohol outcome expectancies. *Behaviour Research and Therapy, 35,* 59–65.

15. Dugas, M. J., Gagnon, F., Ladouceur, R., & Freeston, M. H. (1998). Generalized anxiety disorder: A preliminary test of a conceptual model. *Behaviour Research and Therapy, 36,* 215–226.

16. Pennebaker, J. W., Colder, M., & Sharp, L. K. (1990). Accelerating the coping process. *Journal of Personality and Social Psychology, 58,* 528–537.

17. Weinberger, D. A., Schwartz, G. E., & Davidson, R. J. (1979). Low-anxious, high-anxious, and repressive coping styles: Psychometric patterns and behavioral and physiological responses to stress. *Journal of Abnormal Psychology, 88,* 369–380.

18. Hayes, S. C., Bissett, R., Roget, N., Padilla, M., Kohlenberg, B. S., Fisher, G., et al. (2004). The impact of acceptance and commitment training and multicultural training on the stigmatizing attitudes and professional burnout of substance abuse counselors. *Behavior Therapy, 35,* 821–835.

19. Hayes, S., Luoma, J., Bond, F. W., Masuda, A., & Lillis, J. (2006). Acceptance and Commitment Therapy: Model, processes and outcomes. *Behaviour Research and Therapy, 44,* 1–25.

20. Bond, F. W., & Bunce, D. (2000). Mediators of change in emotion-focused and problem-focused worksite stress management interventions. *Journal of Occupational Health Psychology, 5,* 156–163.

21. Block, J. (2002). *Acceptance and change of private experiences: A comparative analysis in college students with public speaking anxiety.* University of Albany, State University of New York, Albany.

22. Gregg, J. (2004). *A randomized controlled effectiveness trial comparing patient education with and without Acceptance and Commitment Therapy.* University of Nevada, Reno.

23. Dahl, J., Wilson, K. G., & Nilsson, A. (2004). Acceptance and commitment therapy and the treatment of persons at risk for long-term disability resulting from stress and pain symptoms: A preliminary randomized trial. *Behavior Therapy, 35,* 785–801.

24. Beck, J. S. (1995). *Cognitive therapy: Basics and beyond*: New York: Guilford Press.

25. Ellis, A. (2001). *Overcoming destructive beliefs, feelings, and behaviors: New directions for Rational Emotive Behavior Therapy.* Amherst, NY: Prometheus Books.

26. Meichenbaum, D. (1985). *Stress inoculation training.* New York: Pergamon Press.

27. Ciarrochi, J., Robb, H., & Godsell, C. (2005). Letting a little nonverbal air into the room: Insights from Acceptance and Commitment Therapy. Part 1: Philosophical and theoretical underpinnings. *Journal of Rational-Emotive and Cognitive-Behavior Therapy, 23,* 79–106.

28. Ciarrochi, J., & Blackledge, J. T. (in press). Emotional intelligence and interpersonal behaviour: A theory and review of the literature. In J. Forgas (Ed.), *Hearts and minds: Affective influences on social cognition and behaviour.*

29. Coyne, L. W., & Wilson, K. G. (2004). The role of cognitive fusion in impaired parenting: An RFT analysis. *International Journal of Psychology and Psychological Therapy, 4,* 469–486.

30. Hanh, T. N. (1987). *The miracle of mindfulness.* Boston: Beacon Press.
31. Kabat-Zinn, J. (1994). *Wherever you go there you are: Mindfulness meditation in everyday life.* New York: Hyperion.
32. Segal, Z. V., Williams, J. M. G., & Teasdale, J. D. (2002). *Mindfulness-Based Cognitive Therapy for Depression: a new approach to preventing relapse.* New York: Guilford Press.
33. Kapleau, P. (1989). *The three pillars of Zen: Teaching, practice, and enlightenment.* New York: Anchor.
34. Baer, R. A., Smith, G. T., & Allen, K. B. (2004). Assessment of mindfulness by self-report: The Kentucky Inventory of Mindfulness Skills. *Assessment, 11,* 191–206.
35. Brown, K. W., & Ryan, R. M. (2003). The benefits of being present: Mindfulness and its role in psychological well-being. *Journal of Personality and Social Psychology, 84,* 822–848.
36. Ciarrochi, J., Scott, G., Deane, F. P., & Heaven, P. C. L. (2003). Relations between social and emotional competence and mental health: A construct validation study. *Personality and Individual Differences, 35,* 1947–1963.
37. Taylor, G. J. (2000). Recent developments in alexithymia theory and research. *Canadian Journal of Psychiatry, 45,* 134–142.
38. Blackledge, J. T., & Ciarrochi, J. (2005). Assessing values in adolescence. Unpublished manuscript, Wollongong, Australia.
39. Barnes-Holmes, D., Hayes, S., & Barnes-Holmes, Y. (2005). Derived stimulus relations as learned behavior: A modern behavioral approach to human language and cognition. Unpublished manuscript, Kildare, Ireland.
40. Hayes, S. C. (2004). Acceptance and Commitment Therapy, Relational Frame Theory, and the third wave of behavior therapy. *Behavior Therapy, 35,* 639–665.
41. Ciarrochi, J., & Robb, H. (2005). Letting a little nonverbal air into the room: Insights from Acceptance and Commitment Therapy: Part 2: Applications. *Journal of Rational-Emotive and Cognitive Behavior Therapy, 23,* 107–130.
42. Ciarrochi, J. V., Chan, A. Y. C., & Caputi, P. (2000). A critical evaluation of the emotional intelligence construct. *Personality and Individual Differences, 28,* 539–561.
43. Mayer, J. D., Salovey, P., & Caruso, D. R. (2004). Emotional intelligence: Theory, findings, and implications. *Psychological Inquiry, 15,* 197–215.
44. Mayer, J. D., Salovey, P., Caruso, D. R., & Sitarenios, G. (2001). Emotional intelligence as a standard intelligence. *Emotion, 1,* 232–242.
45. Brackett, M. A., & Geher, G. (2006). Measuring emotional intelligence: Paradigmatic diversity and common ground. In J. Ciarrochi, J. Forgas, & J. Mayer (Eds.), *Emotional intelligence in everyday life* (2nd ed., pp. 27–50). New York: Psychology Press.
46. Ciarrochi, J., Forgas, J. P., & Mayer, J. D. (2006). *Emotional intelligence in everyday life: A scientific inquiry* (2nd ed.). New York: Psychology Press.
47. Petrides, K. V., Furnham, A., & Frederickson, N. (2004). Emotional intelligence. *Psychologist, 17,* 574–577.
48. Mayer, J. D., Salovey, P., & Caruso, D. R. (2002). *Mayer-Salovey-Caruso Emotional Intelligence Test (MSCEIT) user's manual.* Toronto, Canada: MHS Publishers.
49. Saarni, C. (1999). *The development of emotional competence*: New York: Guilford Press.

CHAPTER John D. Mayer

Personality Function and Personality Change

In mid-life, Shannon was diagnosed with cancer. She had been a shy child, raised by her mother and stepfather in a trailer park. Her stepfather isolated her and her mother from the rest of the family, told neighbors that his family was crazy, and physically abused his family members. Shannon came to avoid others, labeling herself as shy. No one in their family had attended college, and, after high school, she joined the Navy. In the Navy, she was assigned to a personnel position for which she regularly needed to interact with others. This, in turn, forced her to act in a more outgoing fashion.

While in the Navy, she married – but discovered over time that her husband was both an alcoholic and physically abusive. With help from a crisis center, she divorced him, taking their then 1-year-old son with her across country. After some time, she found a job with the military managing workers in a compensation program, and married and divorced a second time.[1] (pp. 14–16)

Shannon's life to this point suggests that she possessed some considerable strengths, but was struggling with crucial personal issues surrounding her relationships, as well as with challenging life circumstances.[2–5] As a single mother, Shannon went on to manage a workers' compensation program at a military base. In the face of considerable resistance from other personnel, she constructed a set of coherent policies for administering compensation that became a model for that used on other bases. She felt rightfully proud of her accomplishments. Yet her success left her feeling uncomfortably unfulfilled. She felt increasingly troubled by her difficulty in relationships, her lack of education, and her growing economic woes.

Then Shannon was diagnosed with cancer. She thought, "If this is midlife, I don't want to see the rest of it."[1] [(p. 15)] Yet she saw some possibility of change. In addition to the medical help she sought for her cancer, she began to see a counselor who urged her to take stock of her life. With the counselor's help, she began to review her life, and – looking inward to her personality – to recognize her weaknesses, strengths, and to think about how she might go on.

Personality can be defined as the global function of an individual's major psychological subsystems: motivation and emotion, knowledge, the self, and social action. Taking stock involves examining those systems and how they have functioned, along with how well they have served to meet one's goals and desires. Such stock-taking can lead to changes that may promote a better future.

After both medical and psychological treatment, Shannon's cancer went into remission. She perceived her regained health as a defining event of her life, enhancing her sense of independence and achievement, and her connection to a higher power. A further outcome of those events was that, at the counselor's suggestion, she began to attend college classes. Ultimately, she enrolled in a highly prestigious college, and remarked at the time on her belief that her new beginning "will definitely change everything that happens to me from here on out".[1] [(p. 15)] From desperate circumstances, Shannon had succeed in envisioning and creating a life with greater promise.

For many people, personal development involves seeking to strengthen and improve their personalities.[6] By doing so, they hope to surpass self-perceived limitations and to engage in life in a new or renewed fashion. For example, people may notice personality patterns that hold them back – repeated poor choices, or repeated conflicts with others. Taking stock of such repeated patterns can lead to growth, as was the case for Shannon.[1]

An individual may take stock of his or her strengths and weaknesses in many ways. A middle-aged man may review his life story, its ups and downs, and its mistakes and triumphs. On that basis, he may develop a clearer sense of identity. In contrast to the individual, psychologists often are interested in developing general principles that are useful to nearly anyone. A scientific approach begins with a generic understanding of the structure of personality, i.e., what are the key areas of one's personality and how do they interact?

This chapter presents a general description of personality and how it operates, examines some of the techniques developed in psychotherapy practice to improve personality, and then returns to what personality does, with specific attention to how it can be improved. This coverage can be of use in understanding, evaluating, and comparing schools of psycho-therapy, coaching, and other programs that promise personality change.

☐ How Does Personality Work?

To improve personality, it helps to have a broad working model of the system. Practically speaking, there are at least three general approaches to creating an overview of personality. Each of these is of value, but each also has a different emphasis. The first creates an overview according to the psychological traits, such as extraversion and neuroticism, that describe personality. For example, the Big Five trait approach describes personality according to five dimensions: Extraversion, Neuroticism, Openness, Conscientiousness, and Agreeableness.[7,8] This approach tells us about important parts of personality, but without a sense of how the system functions.

A second approach is to divide personalities into types. This approach is promising but is still in an early developmental phase, with its methods, and consequently its findings, still being worked out.[9]

The third approach to personality offers a rich description of personality and how it works. This approach divides personality into broad structures or areas. For example, personality can be divided into areas of motivation, emotion, and cognition, or alternatively into the id, the ego, and the superego,[10–13] and newer more comprehensive divisions are available as well. These divisions then can be used to organize traits according to the structural areas they describe. For example, motivational traits such as the *need for achievement* describe the motivational area; cognitive traits such as *intelligence* describe the cognitive area.

In this third, structural, approach to personality, the divisions of personality help to identify important portions of the system; each area is partly distinct from other areas and, collectively, the areas compre-hensively cover personality's functions. One of the most up-to-date of these divisions of personality is the *systems set*, which divides personality into four areas: energy development, knowledge guidance, conscious self-regulation, and action implementation.[14]

To better understand personality, it helps to go through the structures one by one. This process leads to a sense of the personality system and how its parts operate individually and together, and how the system can be changed and improved. The energy development system will be examined first, for it is here that a person's potential actions begin.

Energy Development

Mental energy can be defined as the potential mental activity people can draw on to function psychologically. People draw on such mental energy to think and act, and are guided by that energy to desire some things and not others. If an individual does not have adequate energy, he or she may be unable to accomplish much, no matter how smart, socially adroit, or self-aware he or she is. Energy levels are crucial to directing an organism's action.

A person's energy development is determined by the level of his or her motives and emotions. As a person's motives rise, the individual will sense energy with which to act; similarly, as his or her coordinated emotions rise, the energy to act becomes more intense still – and may even need to be held back. Motives represent basic urges which propel the person to act. The person experiences urges to eat, drink, engage in sex, and defend his or her territory, among other drives. In human beings, at least, such urges extend to include a person's need for achievement, for power, and for sociability (affiliation).

Motives express only the wants of the individual. Such motivational urges operate independently of what is right or wrong, or even what might work best to attain a goal. In some reptilian species – such as lizards and alligators – motives to stay warm, catch prey, and copulate may be sufficient for survival and reproduction. These animals lay their eggs and move on; they are solitary and do not raise their young. Such a non-social motivational focus is, however, inadequate to guide the lives of mammals, and especially the lives of the mammal *Homo sapiens*.[15,16]

Humans exist in a more complex social reality. Human young are vulnerable and defenseless for an extended period of time, requiring parents to be emotionally attached and protect them. Humans usually need emotional attachments and commitments to each other to survive. In such organisms, motives are joined by a second system that helps to develop energy – the emotions system.

Emotions guide motives by enhancing or discouraging the likelihood of their expression at the right moments. For example, the emotion of anger amplifies the motive of aggression. An emotion such as love will amplify the affiliative motives – to join with others. Sadness encourages isolation.[17]

Emotions emerge at the "right moment" to enhance or discourage a motive because those emotions are a person's internal signals as to the individual's progress in the social world.[18] For example, happiness arises when a friendly remark occurs, and, as such, happiness amplifies affiliative motives at a generally good time for social interaction. Anger arises in response to injustice and that is a time when an aggressive response might be needed.

So, energy development depends on motives and emotions working together. Some co-pairs of motivations and emotions have to do with satisfying underlying biological needs (self-preservation and fear), some with intrapsychic needs (e.g., being happy), others with satisfying social needs (affiliation and love). Energy develops toward specific aims. These aims, in turn, are represented in mental models of how the world works and how to get the things we want in life. These and other functions of energy development are shown in the first row of Table 5.1.

TABLE 5.1. A functional analysis of four areas of personality

Core Functions	Interactive Functions	Outcomes
Energy Development		
• Identify psychobiological urges and desires • Translate biological needs into psychological motives • Attach emotions to motives so as to socially regulate motives • Recognize the interrelation of emotions and their use to regulate (amplify; diminish) motives	• Connect urges and desires to internal representations of aims and goals (with knowledge guidance) • Directly express socially permitted urges and action (e.g., extraversion; introversion) with action implementation • Modulate energy so that it is controllable (with self-control)	• High versus low motivation • Emotionally-blocked versus freely-flowing motivation • Positive versus negative motivational energy • Positive versus negative emotional experience
Knowledge Guidance		
• Develop one's models of the self so as to record one's history and understand one's limits and strengths, and to represent oneself to others • Develop specialized knowledge of the world for advanced and enhanced decision making in key areas • Develop models of others so as to promote healthy outcomes later	• Develop concepts of life possibilities for use in personal planning over time (with self-control) • Develop comprehensive vocational plans that fulfill biological needs while meeting social expectations (with energy development; action implementation) • Develop relationship plans that meet needs and social expectations (with energy development; action implementation)	• Highly knowledgeable versus naïve or ignorant about the world • Good versus bad attitudes about the world • Constructive versus negative thinking styles • Good versus faulty understanding of other people and the social world

Continued

TABLE 5.1.—*continued*

Core Functions	Interactive Functions	Outcomes
Action Implementation • Develop social skills so as to carry out actions effectively • Develop effective skills with which to carry out tasks • Receive social feedback and social rewards • Develop healthy relationship and attachment patterns	• Allow for natural expression of social urges and action (with energy development) • Develop actions in such a way as to promote positive emotions (with energy development; knowledge guidance)	• Natural and genuine social expression versus false and affected expression • Socially skilled versus clumsy and awkward interpersonal activity • Skilled versus unskilled at technical tasks
Conscious Self-Regulation • Sentience • Monitor the time sense and plan in time • Develop self-control	• Intervene in emotional regulation of motives where conscious modifications are required (with energy development) • Monitor changing external conditions for opportunities for more effective, creative action (with action implementation)	• Good self-control versus impulsivity • Strategic versus unclear or abdicated personal planning

Unfortunately, energy development sometimes goes wrong. People plagued by guilt and doubt may find it hard to act under many circumstances. More severely, depressed individuals experience little motivation in any area.[19] A person with many motives and positive emotions, by contrast, will be highly motivated. Some outcomes of energy development are shown in the final column of the energy row.

Knowledge Guidance

Energy development occurs within the context of the person's mental maps or models of the real world. For example, the motive to eat has as its goal of finding food. The notion of food and where it can be found is recorded in the individual's mental models. As another example, sociability has the aim of finding others to be with; those others and their possible behaviors also are recorded in an individual's mental models.

Personality is a psychological system that exists exclusively inside the mind, with no direct contact with outside reality. At the same time it controls a body that does function in an outside world, outside the head. Personality meets reality, in part, through the doors and windows of psychological perception. It receives information through eyes, ears, and touch. In addition, it can test the outside world by directing action in it, and observing the consequence of those acts. Nevertheless psychology is within and other people and objects remain forever outside the skin, beyond personality. These outside agents are, for that reason, known through the individual's mental models only imperfectly.

To be sure, some concrete representations seem real and secure enough. Mental perceptions of stones, rivers, or of a smiling face seem so real that we accept their existence with little question. These representations are near hard-wired representations of the outside world and we navigate them automatically. Motives and emotions attach to these basic representations, and so close are they to reality that we do not usually distinguish *our idea* of a table at which we dine from the physical reality of the table itself. Similarly, we thirst for the river's water, smile at another's smile, and fear the snake, only rarely realizing that we respond to our internal map of each of these, which is but a piece of their total reality. In each instance, the psychological system has produced internal mental indicators of this external reality.

The outside reality of even these day-to-day representations is more complex than perceived. Our thoughts of the river are not the same as the river. If we misread the river's physical reality, we may drown in it. In place of the outside mother, there is an internal representation of mother that is mapped onto incoming sensory signals. In place of the outside home, there is an internal representation of home that is partial.[2,20–23] The six-year-old knows some things about a house: about hiding places and where mom and dad and sister and brother are apt to be, where to find food, where the bathroom is, and the like. The mother and father have a sense of the child's-eye-view of the house, but coupled with that they know all about the appliances, the square footage, the mortgage and how to cover it, and the like. These models – the six-year-old's and the parents' – are both seemingly sufficient for their purposes, yet neither knows all about the home.

A historian may know the age of the house, who owned it 200 years ago, and the owners' part in a political movement. Reality is rich and mental models are always incomplete representations of it. This means that two people may possess substantially different models of a complex entity, and yet each possesses an equally valid representation. As an aside, this is especially true in the realm of ideas. A conservative and a liberal may both start from sound data, and develop well-argued positions from reasonable principles. Both may have equally good – but equally partial – models of the infinitely complex reality. Superficially, they appear to disagree; more deeply, each possesses a partial truth.

Not only are our models incomplete, but they are often systematically incorrect and biased. We distort things to suit our own perspectives.[24] Sometimes the bias goes to the extreme. The paranoid person possesses a cognitive style by which he or she inevitably seeks clues of disloyalty. Because all information is ambiguous, it often is possible to construct a loosely-fitting paranoid theory. It is just that other, non-paranoid models usually fit the facts a bit better.[25]

The things we are motivated to attain in the social world always involve our model of reality rather than the reality itself. The better one's mental models represent the outside world, the more successfully the personality system will operate. Poor or incomplete models will lead to the frustration of the energy development. It is in part for this reason that we often feel slightly disappointed (or worse) at having gained what we wanted. It is, similarly, for this reason that the lover is correct when she says, "you don't love me, you love your image of me."

In contrast, good models will facilitate the success of even weakly developed mental energy. A low-energy person who knows just what she wants and knows exactly how to get it may be extremely effective at taking steps to succeed despite limited energy stores. Moreover, the better our models, the more handsomely they are rewarded by society. People with mental models shaped and developed by extensive formal education earn far more than others.[26] The functions of knowledge guidance, and its outcomes, are summarized in the second row of Table 5.1.

Why are these mental models so important? It is not enough to want to achieve, or even to feel confidence and pride around achieving. If you do not know what you want or how to go about getting it, you are unlikely to meet your needs.

Action Implementation

The individual's mental life takes place in an internal world of mental models that represent reality at one remove. Mental energy develops and is attached to internal mental models. These models correspond to actual goals present in the outside world that may satisfy one's needs. Once goals have been established, the mental system must provide plans for action so as to attain their ends.

Action takes place at various levels of sophistication. At the basic end of this hierarchy are motor skills and actions that are more-or-less automatically expressed by most healthy people past childhood: walking someplace, eating food, shaking hands, smiling as another person passes, and the like.[27]

At the middle and higher stages of social implementation, personality draws on more complex skills. Children with better social skills are better able to join another pair of children who are playing. Socially skilled children ask what is going on and then join in. If two children are playing Batman and Superman, a socially skilled child will say, "Okay, I'll be Spiderman, what are we going to do?" Less socially skilled children are likely to make less relevant remarks. They may say, "My mom is getting me shoes this afternoon."[28]

If one has the energy and the right knowledge, success is probably possible with even minimal social skills. An executive who knows what he wants may attain it, even if he behaves abruptly and without sufficient consideration for others. It helps, however, to be skilled at social implementation. The motivated genius is likely to do better if he or she knows how to maintain friends, contact scientific authorities, and behave appropriately in social situations. Or, as another example, highly attractive people require skills to meet their social needs. An attractive man or woman who lacks social skills to keep away some of those attracted to them, may end up quite unhappy in life, attached to indifferent partners, or making partners they do care about jealous.

Action Implementation and Energy Development

Some people may be high in knowledge and implementation skill but low in the mental energy to carry it out. For example, someone can know what the right action is in a particular situation, and can even demonstrate this right action when it is prudent, as in a job interview, yet rarely put the skills into play when on the job, because he does not regard it as a priority and does not have sufficient energy to carry it out. Some of the characteristics of action implementation are shown in row 3 of Table 5.1, along with some outcomes of this area.

Conscious Self-Regulation

Mental energy can develop, become associated with relevant mental models of the outside world, and generate plans for attaining needed aims, all with little awareness and little self-consciousness. So, a child rehearses tying her shoelaces until finally it requires only minimal concentration. An adult accustomed to a daily commute can drive it with little attention to the surroundings. Sometimes, however, such action can go awry – the person on a diet finds himself opening the jar of chocolate sauce from the refrigerator, or the driver finds herself lost en route.[29–31] In human beings, and perhaps in other animals, there exists a capacity for internal observation, review, and intervention called conscious self-regulation. We possess sentience – a sense of being alive, of mattering, of caring what we think and do.[32–34]

Teaching people the techniques of self-control can alter their behavior and allow them to respond flexibly to difficult situations. As a simple example, teaching children to count to ten before expressing their anger helps provide them with a tool to momentarily inhibit impulsive and regrettable acts, so those acts can be properly evaluated before being expressed. More broadly, it is this consciousness that poses questions such as, "Who shall I be?," "Who shall I become?," and "How shall I change?" Measures such as psychological mindedness and mindfulness may capture some of these qualities.[35]

Self-Regulation and Other Functions

The other areas – energy development, knowledge guidance, and action implementation – all interact with self-regulation. Energy development may direct an individual's function so smoothly as to require little self-control. Knowledge about self-regulation may be superior and guide the person with particularly effective suggestions. Finally, when one wants to regulate a social situation, one may possess excellent social skills with which to do it. Some of these qualities can be found in the final row of Table 5.1.

☐ How is Personality Changed?

Pathways of Change

Each of the four areas of personality described thus far – energy development, knowledge guidance, action implementation, and executive self-control – can be changed and improved. For example, various psychotherapies have developed techniques that affect one area of personality or another. There are, of course, many other influences on the individual, including biopsychological influences such as health and drugs, and social influences including socioeconomic resources, friends, family, peers, and culture. Psychotherapy is among those influences and is unique in being selected by the individual, and in being the subject of considerable study. It is, therefore, better understood than many other change agents.

Some General Aspects of the Therapeutics of Change

Psychotherapy typically involves an interaction between a therapist and a client which is intended to help the client become more psychologically functional and healthy. At first glance, psychotherapy is not specifically aimed at one or another specific part of personality. Psychotherapy often acts in a broad and general way, through common factors – factors that most or all therapies employ. These include, for example, creating a therapeutic relationship, increasing hope, and establishing an expectation of psychological benefit.[36–38] It is also cognitive by nature, because it involves language and instruction.[39]

Specific Effects

Although much of psychotherapy operates by exerting general effects, psychotherapy also is made up of specific change techniques and these techniques do often influence one or more specific areas of personality. A change technique can be defined as "a specific, discrete, and time-limited act, which may involve providing information, directing behavior, or otherwise exerting influence, which is aimed at modifying an aspect of an individual's personality and its expression".[40 (p. 1292)]

An example of such a change technique is the empty-chair technique, which involves asking a client to vividly imagine someone (e.g., one's father) or something (e.g., a wedding ring) in an empty chair and to hold a conversation with that individual or object. Doing so creates an emotionally charged atmosphere and allows the individual to understand how his or her models of other people and the world influence his or her feelings. The empty-chair technique began in a therapy called psychodrama, but later became central to gestalt therapy.[41] Each change technique can be defined and explained apart from any theoretical orientation. These techniques are the building blocks of personality change.

Most change techniques target a particular area of personality. If an individual wishes to enhance her mental energy, for example, several groups of techniques may be particularly helpful. A therapist might try to align a person's goals in a more productive fashion so as to lessen the person's motivational conflicts.[42,43] Or, consider emotional responding: Sometimes the emotion system attaches too much anxiety to an object, and a phobia arises. To remove the phobia, the therapist may employ the technique of systematic desensitization, which substitutes a relaxation response for an anxious one. The individual learns to relax in the presence of increasingly phobic stimuli.

Many therapeutic techniques influence knowledge guidance. Cognitive-behavioral psychologists set out to directly assess and change a person's cognitions about the world. For example, in the *reframing technique*, therapists may examine a person's negative perceptions of a situation and help the individual to see its positive aspects as well. The therapist's hope is that changing the individual's cognitions will activate more positive emotional patterns, and, in turn, facilitate social functioning.

Action implementation more generally involves understanding how to carry out plans in social settings. The technique, *interpreting the transference*, is employed by psychodynamic therapists to point out to an individual his or her maladaptive (or, simply, misguided) behaviors with the therapist. The idea is to indicate repeated patterns of sub-optimal relationships, as they appear in the therapy relationship and elsewhere, and then help the individual to change them.[39,44]

More directly, in Adlerian therapy, therapists help the individual to role-play various social parts, so as to carry them out more effectively. Certainly, many people rehearse stressful social encounters – asking for a raise or asking for a date – ahead of time so as to carry them out more gracefully when the time arises.

Finally, executive self-control, too, can be enhanced. Psychodynamic therapy seeks to accomplish this by placing more of personality under conscious control – that is, by identifying heretofore unnoticed, non-accessed qualities of the self and making them conscious.[44] The technique, *interpreting the defense*, involves the therapist pointing out a person's cognitive avoidance of potentially painful topics (e.g., "I notice that whenever you talk about your brother, you say 'Oh, he's okay' and then move on without considering his presence very much."). As the individual becomes more consciously aware of previously hidden and avoided material, he or she can more clearly think about it and exercise judicious control over its influence. Contemporary research often focuses on evaluating approaches to self-control so as to identify techniques with the potential to enhance an individual's executive governance.[45]

☐ How Can Personality be Improved?

Improving the Personality System

An individual's personality attempts to satisfy the person's biological needs in a social context. These needs can be relatively basic, such as with food and drink, or more complex, including concerns for safety, esteem, and love. The individual may be trying to assert some sense of unique individuality or to fulfill – to actualize – his or her sense of self. All the parts of personality – energy development, knowledge guidance, action implementation, and executive consciousness – cooperate in these goals.

Yet, the developmental plan for each individual will be different. Each person has a different genetic endowment, a different set of skills and qualities, a different family, and different values . . . The individual may live in an individualistic or a communitarian culture. Moreover, personality is typically, by comparison with the biological and social systems around it, a relatively weak system, bobbing about in an ocean of potentially threatening or promising current events and influences. It should be clear that optimizing personality will depend in part upon the individual's context, that is, *actualization can be defined in different ways by different people.* A person can be actualized according to his or her skills or motives, according to others' wishes, according to society's needs, or according to some global zeitgeist, religion, or philosophy.

The systems set offers some simplifications and approximations that, although inadequate to capture the individual's full complexity, may nevertheless be helpful. Each area of personality can be improved, and as each is improved different advantages occur. For example, improving energy development means developing motivations that will help the individual, or means helping to fulfill the individual's already-existing adaptive needs. It means developing good emotional reactions to situations, and tying them to those better motivations. For example, a man who believes that he is not worth very much may allow his supervisor to order him around, which, in turn, makes him feel further depressed and deprives him of rewards. By re-rigging his energy development, he may learn that he is worth more and uncover a motive (and the accompanying social skills) to assert himself appropriately.

As regards mental models, improvement here involves creating more accurate models of the world. Mental models of significant others, friends, spouses, and the like, all may need development in individuals who come from troubled home environments. Psychotherapeutic practices and group psychotherapy may be of some assistance in such instances. For example, a woman whose father was an alcoholic and spoke down to her might develop an attraction to being in such a relationship again as an adult. To avoid this, she may need to create new models of men before marrying, so as to be able to connect emotionally to healthy men and to learn the behaviors useful for healthy relationships. For many people, the *main event* here is one of education (consider Shannon in the opening case). The use of school systems and institutions of higher learning to create more accurate, efficient mental models of the world is well known, and the value added to the individual hardly needs to be restated in an information age. At the same time, people also possess mental models that are not developed or examined in such institutions, such as the models one creates for potential friends and spouses. Both psychotherapy and programs such as those discussed in this book address these other more informal models.

Next, there is the issue of action implementation. Simply recognizing the urge to be more independent of one's supervisor and developing mental models of better ways to relate to people is not enough. A person must have decent ways of expressing the matter socially. Saying to the supervisor "You are running all over me and I am sick of it," may possibly be effective but it is risky and non-optimal. Developing a more considered plan of action – taking into account the conditions at work and the personality of the supervisor and potential opportunities for tact – will be far more likely to bring about a positive outcome in some instances.

Finally, to do all this means exerting self-control: resisting destructive impulses, and waiting until one knows enough and understands what one wants to do and the risks involved. This requires understanding the situation and oneself and electing to change.

The Nature of Personality Change

Personality is a slow-to-express, slow-to-change system. To be sure, short-term dramatic alterations in personality do take place. Even these brief, dramatic changes may be manifestations of longer-term changes that have built up and then are revealed quickly. The sorts of linear, predictable changes mostly studied by psychologists, however, suggest that long-term slow change is the norm.

Consider the persistence of IQ. A group of preschool children's IQs will correlate $r = .86$ with their own re-assessed IQs measured one year later ($r = .77$ at two years) and still be $r = .59$ after 25 years.[46,47] These correlations indicate that, although people's relative standing on IQ changes over time, such changes arise gradually. The stability of aggression is similar to that of IQ.[48]

As stable as personality is, its influence in any given situation also is quite modest. Most reviews conclude that traits predict individual behaviors in the 10–15% range.[49,50] Small, next to invisible changes nonetheless are likely to accumulate over time, and to have effects on a person's long-term future.[51,52]

This pattern of slow change and gradual influence is likely to explain why attempts at personality change take time. Assuming that a client sees a psychotherapist once a week, only 25% of clients will be detectably improved after 2 months (8 sessions), 50% will show improvement between 3 and 4 months (13 to 18 sessions), and 75% will show improvement after 6 months (26 sessions).[53,54] Interestingly, survey studies indicate that most people receive only five sessions of psychotherapy, which is not nearly long enough to experience much gain.[53] Patience – even resigned patience – is called for when considering one's own personality. Over time, the rewards of positive improvement, modest though they may be, are likely to become evident – and can gradually make a positive impact on one's social relationships and well-being. For example, if personality accounts for 10% or 15% of the variance of a decision, or the outcome of a situation, those small influences can add up appreciably over a period of time, impacting a person's life dramatically.

☐ Summary and Conclusions

People seek help for many reasons, but chief among them are personal distress along with hope and faith in the possibility of improving who they are.[55] Usually, people enter into an agreement to undergo change so as to feel better and act more effectively when pursuing goals.[56]

This article sketched a view of the personality system as consisting of four major areas of processing: energy development, knowledge guidance, action implementation, and executive self-control. Each of those four areas carries out crucial functions. When those functions go awry, certain problematic outcomes specific to the given area can be observed. For example (and a bit simplistically), depression can indicate an issue with disrupted energy development. Alternatively, impulsivity may indicate issues with executive self-control. Other possible signals of a malfunctioning personality system are shown in Table 5.2 (second column).

When a person desires to change a part of personality for the better, there are usually several alternatives for doing so. Various change techniques exist for each area of personality and many such techniques have been employed and studied in the context of psychotherapy, and sometimes in other contexts as well. Techniques evaluated as effective also are likely to be useful in the context of career counseling, executive development, and in other more personal relationships as well.

When considering a program of change, be it psychotherapy or executive coaching, it helps to consider the areas of personality that are most critically impacted and that require the most change, and then the techniques possible for bringing about such change. For example, coaching programs such as the ones in this volume can impact many areas of the personality systems in a positive fashion. The third column of

TABLE 5.2. Areas of personality and change goals

Area	Motivation for Change	Change Goals
Energy Development	• Low energy • Unhappiness and negativity	• Higher, more sustained levels of mental energy • More positive mental energy directed more constructively
Knowledge Guidance	• Invalid, naïve models of the self and world • Negative views of the self and world	• More accurate and realistic mental models • More constructive mental models
Action Implementation	• Poor social skills • Negative social impact	• Better talents and skills • More positive social contributions
Executive Control	• Distracted, limited conscious experience • Impulsivity or overly rigid self-control	• Better organized, more mindful consciousness • Flexible, efficient self-control

Table 5.2 illustrates some of the change goals that are relevant to each of the major areas of personality.

The relative stability of personality, its modest power of expression from situation to situation, and the time it takes to change mean that an individual should not expect change right away, but rather must look for small changes over time. Change certainly does arise over time. Although patience is needed, the rewards can be great.

☐ References

1. Wentworth, P., & Peterson, B. E. (2001). Crossing the line: Studies of identity development in first-generation college women. *Journal of Adult Development, 8*, 9–21.
2. Andersen, S. M., & Berk, M. S. (1998). Transference in everyday experience: Implications of experimental research for relevant clinical phenomena. *Review of General Psychology, 2*, 81–120.
3. Banyard, V. I., Williams, L. M., & Siegal, J. A. (2001). The long-term mental health consequences of child sexual abuse: An exploratory study of multiple traumas in a sample of women. *Journal of Traumatic Stress, 14*, 697–715.
4. Bartholomew, K., & Horowitz, L. M. (1991). Attachment styles among young adults: A test of a four-category model. *Journal of Personality and Social Psychology, 61*, 226–244.
5. Leitenberg, H., Gibson, L. E., & Novy, P. L. (2004). Individual differences among undergraduate women in methods of coping with stressful events: The impact of cumulative childhood stressors and abuse. *Child Abuse and Neglect, 28*, 181–192.

6. Helson, R., & Srivastava, S. (2001). Three paths of adult development: Conservers, seekers, and achievers. *Journal of Personality and Social Psychology, 80*, 995–1010.
7. Goldberg, L. R. (1993). The structure of phenotypic personality traits. *American Psychologist, 48*, 26–34.
8. McCrae, R. R., & Costa, P. T., Jr. (1999). A five-factor theory of personality. In L. A. Pervin & O. P. John (Eds.), *Handbook of personality: Theory and research* (2nd ed., pp. 139–153). New York/London: Guilford Press.
9. Cronbach, L. J., & Meehl, P. E. (1955). Construct validity in psychological tests. *Psychological Bulletin, 52*, 281–302.
10. Bellak, L., Hurvich, M., & Gediman, H. (1973). *Ego functions in schizophrenics, neurotics, and normals.* New York: John Wiley & Sons.
11. Boesky, D. (1994). Dialogue on the Brenner paper between Charles Brenner, M.D., and Dale Boesky, M.D. *Journal of Clinical Psychoanalysis, 3*, 509–522.
12. Brenner, C. (1994). The mind as conflict and compromise formation. *Journal of Clinical Psychoanalysis, 3*, 473–488.
13. Hilgard, E. R. (1980). The trilogy of mind: Cognition, affection, and conation. *Journal of the History of the Behavioral Sciences, 16*, 107–117.
14. Mayer, J. D. (2005). A tale of two visions: Can a new view of personality help integrate psychology? *American Psychologist, 60*, 294–307.
15. MacLean, P. D. (1990). *The triune brain in evolution: Role in the paleocerebral functions.* New York: Plenum Press.
16. Smith, C. P., Atkinson, J. W., McClelland, D. C., & Veroff, J. (1992). *Motivation and personality: Handbook of thematic content analysis.* New York: Cambridge University Press.
17. Tomkins, S. S. (1984). Affect theory. In K. R. Scherer & P. Ekman (Eds.), *Approaches to emotion* (2nd ed., pp. 353–395). Hillsdale, NJ: Lawrence Erlbaum Associates, Inc.
18. Mayer, J. D., & Salovey, P. (1997). What is emotional intelligence? In P. Salovey & D. Sluyter (Eds.), *Emotional development and emotional intelligence: Educational implications* (pp. 3–31). New York: Basic Books.
19. Beck, A. T., Rush, A. J., Shaw, B. F., & Emery, G. (1979). *Cognitive therapy of depression.* New York: Guilford Press.
20. Cantor, N., & Mischel, W. (1977). Traits as prototypes: Effects on recognition memory. *Journal of Personality and Social Psychology, 35*, 38–48.
21. Kelly, G. A. (1955). *The psychology of personal constructs. Volume One: A theory of personality.* New York: W. W. Norton.
22. Mayer, J. D., Rapp, H. C., & Williams, L. (1994). Individual differences in behavioral prediction: The acquisition of personal-action schemata. *Personality and Social Psychology Bulletin, 19*, 443–451.
23. Singer, J. L. (1985). Transference and the human condition: A cognitive-affective perspective. *Psychoanalytic Quarterly, 2*, 189–219.
24. Greenwald, A. G. (1980). The totalitarian ego: Fabrication and revision of personal history. *American Psychologist, 35*, 603–618.
25. Shapiro, D. (1965). *Neurotic styles.* Oxford, UK: Basic Books.
26. Cheeseman Day, J., & Neuberger, E. C. (2002). *The big payoff: Educational attainment and synthetic estimates of work-life earnings.* US Bureau of the Census, Special Reports [P23-210]. Washington, DC: US Government Printing Office.
27. Mayer, J. D. (2003). Structural divisions of personality and the classification of traits. *Review of General Psychology, 7*, 381–401.
28. Black, B., & Hazen, N. L. (1990). Social status and patterns of communication in acquainted and unacquainted preschool children. *Developmental Psychology, 26*, 379–387.
29. Bowers, K. S. (1984). On being unconsciously influenced and informed. In K. S. Bowers

& D. Meichenbaum (Eds.), *The unconscious reconsidered* (pp. 227–272). New York: John Wiley & Sons.

30. Dennett, D. C. (1978). Toward a cognitive theory of consciousness. In D. C. Dennett (Ed.), *Brainstorms: Philosophical essays on mind and psychology* (pp. 149–173). Cambridge, MA: MIT Press.

31. Kihlstrom, J. F. (1987). The cognitive unconscious. *Science, 237,* 1445–1452.

32. Ornstein, R. (1986). *The psychology of consciousness.* New York: Penguin Books.

33. Pinker, S. (1997). *How the mind works.* New York: W. W. Norton.

34. Pribram, K. H. (1978). Consciousness: A scientific approach. *Journal of Indian Psychology, 1,* 95–118.

35. McCallum, M., & Piper, W. E. (1997). *Psychological mindedness: A contemporary understanding.* Mahwah, NJ: Lawrence Erlbaum Associates, Inc.

36. Frank, J. D., & Frank, J. B. (1991). *Persuasion and healing: A comparative study of psychotherapy* (3rd ed.). Baltimore: Johns Hopkins University Press.

37. Messer, S. B. (2001). Empirically supported treatments: What's a non-behaviorist to do? In B. D. Slife, R. N. Williams, & S. H. Barlow (Eds.), *Critical issues in psychotherapy. Translating new ideas into practice* (pp. 3–19). Thousand Oaks, CA: Sage.

38. Nathan, P. E., Stuart, S. P., & Dolan, S. L. (2000). Research on psychotherapy efficacy and effectiveness: Between Scylla and Charybdis? *Psychological Science, 126,* 961–981.

39. Piper, W. E., McCallum, M., Joyce, A. S., Azim, H. F., & Ogrodniczuk, J. S. (1999). Follow-up findings for interpretive and supportive forms of psychotherapy and patient personality variables. *Journal of Consulting and Clinical Psychology, 67,* 267–273.

40. Mayer, J. D. (2004). Classifying change techniques according to the areas of personality they influence: A systems framework integration. *Journal of Clinical Psychology, 60,* 1291–1315.

41. Wulf, R. (1998). The historical roots of Gestalt therapy. *Gestalt Journal, 21,* 81–93.

42. Klinger, E., & Cox, W. M. (2004). Motivation and the theory of current concerns. In W. M. Cox & E. Klinger (Eds.), *Handbook of motivational counseling* (pp. 3–27). Chichester, UK: John Wiley & Sons.

43. Michalak, J., Heidenreich, T., & Hoyer, J. (2004). Goal conflicts: Concepts, findings, and consequences for psychotherapy. In W. M. Cox & E. Klinger (Eds.), *Handbook of motivational counseling* (pp. 83–98). Chichester, UK: John Wiley & Sons.

44. Weiner, I. B. (1975). *Principles of psychotherapy.* New York: John Wiley & Sons.

45. Fredrickson, B. L., & Losada, M. F. (2005). Positive affect and the complex dynamics of human flourishing. *American Psychologist, 60,* 678–686.

46. Bradway, K. P., Thompson, C. W., & Cravens, R. B. (1958). Preschool IQs after twenty-five years. *Journal of Educational Psychology, 49,* 278–281.

47. Primrose, A. F., Fuller, M., & Littledyke, M. (2000). Verbal reasoning test scores and their stability over time. *Educational Research, 42,* 167–174.

48. Olweus, D. (1979). Stability of aggressive reaction patterns in males: A review. *Psychological Bulletin, 86,* 852–875.

49. Funder, D. C. (2001). *The personality puzzle.* New York: W. W. Norton.

50. Mischel, W. (1968). *Personality and assessment.* New York: John Wiley & Sons.

51. Epstein, S. (1980). The stability of behavior: II. Implications for psychological research. *American Psychologist, 35,* 790–806.

52. Epstein, S. (1983). Aggregation and beyond: Some basic issues on the prediction of behavior. *Journal of Personality, 51,* 360–392.

53. Hansen, N. B., Lambert, M. J., & Forman, E. M. (2002). The psychotherapy dose-response effect and its implications for treatment delivery services. *Clinical Psychology: Science and Practice, 9,* 329–343.

54. Howard, K. I., Kopta, M. S., Krause, M. S., & Orlinsky, D. E. (1986). The dose–effect relationship in psychotherapy. *American Psychologist, 41,* 159–164.

55. Grencavage, L. M. N., & John, C. (1990). Where are the commonalities among the therapeutic common factors? *Professional Psychology: Research and Practice, 21,* 372–378.
56. Leong, F. T. L., & Zachar, P. (1999). Gender and opinions about mental illness as predictors of attitudes toward seeking professional psychological help. *British Journal of Guidance and Counselling, 27,* 123–132.

6
CHAPTER

Joseph Ciarrochi
John D. Mayer

The Key Ingredients of Emotional Intelligence Interventions: Similarities and Differences

In four chapters, psychologists with highly regarded change programs in EI have described how they help people enhance their social, emotional, and personal functioning. Their four programs come from different perspectives, rely on different theories, and likely create different sorts of change.

The four programs involve the school-based emotional intelligence (EI) intervention of Brackett and Katulak (Chapter 1), the managerial emotional competence intervention of Boyatzis (Chapter 2), the workplace EI intervention of Kornacki and Caruso (Chapter 3), and the Mindfulness-Based Emotional Intelligence Training (MBEIT) of Ciarrochi, Blackledge, Bilich, and Bayliss (Chapter 4).

In this chapter, we review and compare the four programs. Some of the similarities and differences among programs are fairly easy to keep in mind. For example, with the exception of the Brackett and Katulak work (Chapter 1), which concerns children, all the rest are focused on adults. Moreover, the work by Boyatzis and by Kornacki and Caruso is primarily addressed to adults at work.

There are, however, other differences. In this brief chapter, we will compare the approaches as to theory, to techniques of change, and to plausibility of their effectiveness.

☐ Theory

The approaches come from quite different theoretical orientations. The Brackett and Katulak program, as well as the program by Kornacki and Caruso, most closely deal with EI as a focused ability. Both of these programs are based on the four-branch model of Mayer and Salovey,[1] which states that EI involves the accurate perception of emotion, the use of emotion to facilitate thought, understanding emotion, and managing emotion. Both programs follow that outline, though in different ways. The Brackett and Katulak program, for example, teaches those four areas, whereas the Kornacki and Caruso program integrates the four areas in a stepwise progression of learning that can be used, and enriched, over a person's ongoing, repeated, work interactions.

The Boyatzis and Ciarrochi programs are, arguably, more general in scope and aim toward a more general coaching effect – one that extends beyond EI proper. Although this is true of the earlier programs as well, these latter two programs appear more focused on personality development than on EI specifically. What they both have in common is their goal of promoting behavior that stays value congruent, even in the context of intense, negative emotions (what Ciarrochi terms "emotionally intelligent behavior," see Chapter 4). The Boyatzis program is largely derived from Intentional Change Theory. This theory posits that people go through a sequence of discoveries, which help them to become more socially and emotionally effective and to develop and move toward an ideal self.

The Ciarrochi program is based on the theories of Hayes and colleagues, which posit that ordinary language processes and experiential avoidance contribute to people becoming socially and emotionally effective. The theory posits concrete manipulations for undermining an individual's potentially harmful use of language and avoidance – and moving them toward greater mindfulness and psychological health.

☐ Techniques

The four interventions described in this book employ a variety of techniques that are both interesting and creative. One can always create a "novel" intervention that, however, uses established procedures and adds functionally trivial "bells and whistles."[2] For that reason, it is often productive to evaluate the known mechanisms of change within those interventions.[2–4] Once we identify the mechanisms, then we can evaluate each one to see if it is effective (i.e., does better than a placebo condition). Effective mechanisms then can be added to an intervention, and ineffective ones dropped. In this way, intervention research can create progressively better interventions rather than evaluating an endless array of therapeutic packages.

We have informally divided the techniques into two broad areas: those aimed at enhancing EI within the framework of the four-branch model,[1] and those aimed at enhancing social and emotional functioning more generally (See also Chapter 5 on "Personality Function and Personality Change" for more on this approach.) In this chapter, techniques that address the four-branch model are organized branch-by-branch into perception, using, understanding, and managing emotions. The personality area is divided into effective emotional orientation, defusion, value clarification, value instruction, increasing the amount and accuracy of self-feedback, and increasing knowledge of effective and ineffective behaviors.

Techniques Aimed Specifically at Emotional Intelligence, as Conceptualized by the Mayer and Salovey Ability Model

We begin with a group of techniques that are especially focused on emotional knowledge and skill.

Techniques to Enhance Identifying Emotions

Every socioemotional learning (SEL) program we are aware of targets emotional identification. It seems to be central to the interventions based on the school-based and workplace EI interventions. For example, the school-based EI intervention helps students to gain a holistic understanding of feeling words by teaching them emotion labels and then encouraging them to apply these labels across a number of contexts (e.g., real world situations, family situations). They also may explore feeling words in creative writing tasks. The programs by Brackett and Katulak for children and Kornacki and Caruso for adults at work both have extensive exercises based on improving such skills.

The managerial emotional competence intervention (Chapter 2) emphasizes not just emotional awareness but also accurate awareness of one's own competencies. The intervention increases awareness by having people engage in a variety of activities and provide extensive feedback on how they performed. Other SEL programs also target awareness in general, rather than focusing on awareness of emotions per se.[5]

Mindfulness-based EI training (MBEIT) helps people to become mindfully aware of emotions as they occur. One exercise involves asking people to close their eyes and imagine leaves floating by on a stream. Once people have this image in their head, they are instructed to watch for emotions, thoughts, and images that show up. As each one shows up, they are to place it on a leaf and watch it go by on the stream. The presumption is that once people become aware of emotions, they are better able to identify them.

Techniques to Enhance Using Emotion to Facilitate Thought

Using emotion involves the ability to recognize what emotions are best for different situations, to harness emotional energy to facilitate thinking and behavior, and to generate optimal emotional states for different contexts. This seems to be most clearly targeted in the school-based and workplace EI interventions and less so in the other interventions. For example, Kornacki and Caruso's workplace EI intervention illustrates how to influence other people's emotions, and teaches people which emotions are ideally suited for different types of activities. For example, happy mood is ideally suited for creative activities like brainstorming.

An interesting disagreement regarding such interventions concerns the four-branch model view of using emotion[1] and the mindfulness-based (MBEIT) view of Ciarrochi. The latter regards attempts to generate particular emotional states as often problematic (Chapter 4). Rather, MBEIT encourages people to learn to accept whatever emotions show up during the course of engaging in a valued activity. Thus, they might learn to feel sad and engage in brainstorming.

Naturally, given its theoretical outlook, MBEIT does not teach the generation of emotional states, but it does not assume that such attempts are always ineffective. It may be that in some circumstances generating emotions is helpful, and in other circumstances, it is unhelpful. Future research can help to decide if that is the case, and, if so, when using a given approach is best.

Techniques to Enhance Emotional Understanding

This area involves understanding the causes of emotions in oneself and others, and understanding how they progress and transform over time. Again, both Brackett and Katulak's and Kornacki and Caruso's interventions address this area. For example, both interventions ask people to engage in a number of activities that help them to recognize the situations that elicit particular emotions.

In contrast, Boyatzis' managerial emotional competence intervention is likely to indirectly target this dimension by helping people to become aware of what they and others are feeling in certain critical situations, and to understand when others become anxious or angry. This necessitates using and clarifying emotional vocabulary. Ciarrochi's mindfulness-based

(MBEIT) approach also is likely to indirectly target this dimension by increasing mindful awareness of emotions as they occur, which should help people to notice the causes of emotions and how they progress over time (see description of mindfulness exercise above). These speculations need to be tested empirically. It is possible that the more indirect approach of these latter two programs may not target this dimension as effectively as more direct techniques.

Emotional Management

This dimension involves attempts to *directly* alter the form and frequency of emotions. It includes attempts to increase or decrease emotions by, for example, exercise, challenging aversive beliefs in order to make them more positive or accurate, building optimism, or increasing self-esteem. Three of the EI and SEL models have this as a component, usually under the label of "managing emotions," or "thinking optimistically."

For example, in the school-based EI intervention, teachers are encouraged to brainstorm about and record possible strategies they could implement to manage their negative emotions. Such strategies include self-talk, exercise, talking to a friend or colleague, and deep-breathing. Kornacki and Caruso's workplace EI intervention teaches people to generate particular moods by having them think of the details of a situation that elicits the mood. Boyatzis' managerial intervention (Chapter 2) seeks to increase emotional self-control by providing people with feedback on how they perform in emotionally difficult situations. The extent to which this kind of behavioral feedback targets frequency of emotions (e.g., does it help people to feel less anger?) versus targeting the function of that private experience (e.g., does anger no longer lead to destructive behavior?; see next section) is unknown. Ciarrochi's mindfulness approach again takes a somewhat contrary approach on emotion management, not actively teaching self-intervention or control techniques, and in many circumstances actively discouraging it (see the sections on emotional orientation and defusion below).

More General Positive Personality Change

Emotional skills develop in the context of a personality more generally. Much of what has been examined thus far concerns a person's development of emotional responding and knowledge. Yet most of the applied practices here include techniques that influence personality beyond its specifically emotional functioning. We view that as an advantage because no part of an individual's psychology operates in isolation. Here we continue the discussion with an examination of techniques that influence other parts of personality. What all these techniques have in common is that they are designed to promote personal development, often with a focus on effective behavior and life strategies.

Techniques that Promote Effective Emotional Orientation

Effective emotional orientation involves the extent to which people are willing to experience unpleasant emotions and emotionally charged thoughts and images, if doing so will help them to move in a valued direction (see Chapter 4 for more detail). "Being willing" means having emotions, without trying to change them, even when they are extremely unpleasant, and even when they are leading to unhelpful cognitive biases. Ineffective emotional orientation involves the tendency to change or chronically suppress unpleasant private experience in a way that inter-feres with valued living. For example, people with post-traumatic stress disorder will frequently go to great lengths to avoid situations that elicit their traumatic memory. Consequently, they may avoid people and places that are important to them, even though such avoidance does not eliminate the distressing memories and may even make them worse.[6]

Effective emotional orientation is a central process targeted in Ciarrochi's MBEIT, with about 25% of the intervention spent on this. For example, one exercise involves having people list all the strategies that they have used to change distress. Then, they are asked to reflect on the extent that the strategies work, i.e., that they are successfully able to eliminate distress. A frequent outcome of this exercise is that people come to recognize that they have been trying for years, without success, to get rid of their distress. They come to recognize the hopelessness of the emotional control agenda. Ideally, they also start to see that letting go of control can free up energy to commit to valued living (e.g., you do not have to wait till you make yourself feel confident in order to get started on a valued activity).

Effective orientation is undoubtedly targeted to some extent by the other interventions as well. For example, the school-based and workplace EI interventions support the importance of emotion by teaching that it conveys valuable information. Whilst Ciarrochi and his colleagues (MBEIT, Chapter 4) consider emotional orientation to be distinct from emotion management, and even opposed to it, other researchers may consider orientation to be a part of emotion management. For example, they may teach effective emotional orientation, with the goal of reducing negative affect (emotion management).

Techniques that Promote Defusion

Defusion was described in the MBEIT chapter. It involves skills that help one to undermine the unhelpful function of emotions and thoughts. For example, in a fused context, if someone says, "You are stupid," you may feel emotional pain and decide not to engage in an intelligent behavior. Thus, "you are stupid" has a controlling role over behavior. In a defused context, in contrast, the same verbal sequence can be experienced as sounds, as a foreign language, and consequently has little or no impact on your feelings or behavior. In general, thoughts and feelings do not have to be viewed as causes for other behaviors, and therefore do not have to be eliminated to effect a change in overt behavior.[6] Rather, one can manipulate the context in which thoughts and emotions occur, so that they no longer have an unhelpful controlling role over behavior.

Ciarrochi's MBEIT teaches people a variety of skills designed to help them defuse from unhelpful emotions and thoughts. The most prominent techniques involve increased mindfulness skills, or the ability of people to take a non-judgmental, observer perspective on their thoughts and feelings. This perspective is hypothesized to help people to experience thoughts and feelings for what they are, fleeting sounds and sensations, and not what they seem to be, e.g., dangers or facts that must dictate behavior. For example, a client may be instructed to mindfully observe her feelings of anxiety and her evaluations, such as "I'm not good enough." She learns to let the anxiety and evaluations come and go, without taking them too seriously, and without allowing the anxiety to dictate her behavior.

MBEIT focuses on defusion perhaps more than any other program.[6] Other approaches probably also target defusion. Essentially, any intervention that helps people to act effectively, when they are feeling a disturbing thought, is targeting the unhelpful functions of that thought (i.e., is targeting defusion). For example, the interventions in this book are likely to help people to act effectively, even when they are feeling angry.

The critical distinction between the MBEIT and the other approaches is that MBEIT centrally focuses on the acceptance of emotions and discourages attempts to change them. Thus, defusion is not used to control feelings. It is specifically about helping people to act better, even when they are experiencing strong emotions. Clients do not learn to alter the frequency of negative emotions or the content of the emotions (e.g., by positive self-talk or engaging in deep breathing). They learn to fully experience distressing emotions *and* to act effectively.

Techniques that Involve Value Clarification

Values can be defined as "verbally construed global life conse-quences".[6] [(p. 206)] They allow one to represent long-term life directions, stay committed to those long-term directions, and resist more immediate impulses. In Ciarrochi's MBEIT program, values are central to the ability to engage in emotionally intelligent behavior and effective behavior more generally. Values serve as a compass during emotionally difficult times, allowing you to behave effectively, even if emotions try to "push" you in an opposite direction. For example, if you value good relations with people, then you can act in a way that facilitates this value (i.e., compromise if needed), even when angry.

Value clarification is a strong component of Ciarrochi's MBEIT (Chapter 4) and Boyatzis' managerial emotional competence intervention (Chapter 2). It is understandably less directly targeted by the workplace and school-based EI interventions as these focus more specifically on emotional learning. However, these interventions may indirectly increase value clarity, by getting people to focus on the utility of behaviors (e.g., by asking, "is this behavior taking you where you want to go?").

Techniques that Increase Ethical, Prosocial Behavior

Another class of interventions in these programs seeks to alter people's values to make them more pro-social or ethical. Such interventions are a common component of SEL programs more generally[5] but appear to be relatively de-emphasized in the chapters in this book. Examples include interventions that encourage people to experience empathy, to engage in safe, legal, and/or ethical behaviors, to respect others, and to appreciate diversity.[5] Ciarrochi's MBEIT and Boyatzis' managerial competence programs allow people to identify and clarify their own values, and appear to minimize manipulations that alter the content of values. Research is needed to evaluate the extent that direct attempts to increase pro-social values actually result in more pro-social behaviors. The success of SEL programs in promoting more pro-social behaviors may be due to any one of many components that are in the SEL program.[7]

Techniques that Increase the Amount of Accuracy and Self-Feedback

This type of intervention teaches people to engage in life experiments and to set up situations where they can receive experiential feedback on the effectiveness of their behavior. The Boyatzis managerial intervention presents the clearest example of this ingredient. It actively encourages people to discover new behaviors, thoughts, and feelings via life experiments. MBEIT also emphasizes utilizing experience to guide behavior, rather than relying excessively on verbally generated rules and evaluations.

Techniques that Directly Increase Knowledge of Effective and Ineffective Behaviors

Some further interventions seek to teach people directly about what behaviors are socially effective and ineffective. For example, they may teach people how to assert themselves effectively (e.g., "focus your complaint on the behavior, rather than personality or the individual"). This component is represented in Boyatzis' managerial intervention, which helps people to create a learning agenda that identifies skill weaknesses and ways to address them.

It is possible that both Brackett and Katulak's school-based program and Kornacki and Caruso's workplace EI interventions target this component to some extent. Specifically, the emotion management component of these interventions appears to target two major factors: the frequency or intensity of certain emotions, and the occurrence of emotionally driven, unhelpful behaviors. In carrying out such teaching, it may implicitly communicate what sorts of emotionally charged behaviors are and are not likely to be effective.

☐ Research Evidence Related to Intervention Processes

The majority of research has evaluated entire intervention packages, and has not sought to separately evaluate the change techniques and more general educational processes of the package. The individual chapters in this book have presented evidence that supports the utility of the respective intervention package, and this evidence will not be repeated here. Below, we describe, in a brief, non-comprehensive fashion, a few pieces of evidence that exist – and indicate some research that may be needed – in support of the individual components in the interventions. The literature on clinical therapy techniques and outcomes is vast and the following comments are, at best, suggestive of the status of the techniques employed here.

Emotional Identification

There is substantial evidence that having difficulty identifying emotions is linked to poor emotional well-being and social difficulties.[8-10] Experimental research is needed to examine whether interventions that focus exclusively on increasing emotion identification skills lead to actual increases in emotion identification and to improvements in social and emotional well-being.

Emotion Management

There is evidence for the benefits of teaching emotion management strategies, such as deep breathing, cognitive restructuring, and reframing.[11] For example, traditional cognitive-behavioral therapy (CBT) teaches one to challenge unhelpful thoughts (e.g., "I am worthless"), and replace these thoughts with more helpful thoughts (e.g., "I am a person of worth"), in order to reduce anxiety, depression, and anger. CBT packages have found substantial empirical support.[11] However, these packages typically involve many ingredients in addition to emotion management (e.g., behavioral activation; exposure; the therapeutic relationship). It is always possible that one of these other ingredients is responsible for the beneficial effects. For example, Jacobsen and his colleagues have shown that one can eliminate the cognitive structuring component of CBT interventions and still show improvements in emotional functioning.[12] This study does not refute the value of cognitive restructuring. Rather, it casts doubt on whether such a component is *necessary* for improvement. Future research is needed to evaluate the extent that emotion management interventions like cognitive restructuring are both effective and necessary.

Defusion

As conceptualized in Ciarrochi's MBEIT, defusion interventions seek to change the unhelpful function of emotions and thoughts, rather than changing the form of these private experiences (as happens with emotion management interventions). Some research suggests that intervention that focuses exclusively on defusion can be effective.[13] However, most of the research involving defusion has evaluated defusion in a much larger intervention package, which involved many intervention ingredients.[14] Future research is needed to evaluate the extent that defusion, by itself, is effective.

Emotional Orientation

As reviewed in the chapter on MBEIT, there is clear evidence that effective emotional orientation is related to positive social and emotional well-being outcomes. In addition, there is reasonable evidence that interventions can increase emotional orientation, and that such increases lead to improvements in emotional well-being.[6,15]

Exposure is one of the most empirically supported interventions in clinical psychology and is likely to increase effective emotional orientation.[16] Exposure involves presenting a client with anxiety-producing material (or other distressing material) for sufficient duration or frequency so as to decrease the intensity of their emotional reaction. Exposure may help people to learn the benefit of facing fears, rather than avoiding them.

Values and Behavioral Activation

Research suggests that happier people tend to hold values for intrinsic rather than extrinsic reasons, tend to engage in valued behavior that is challenging but not "too" challenging, and tend to successfully commit to and put values into play.[17,18] Other research suggests that getting people to engage in enjoyable activities leads to decreases in depression.[12] Additional research is needed to evaluate whether value clarification, by itself, is an active ingredient in interventions.

Utilization and Understanding Emotions

The key components of Mayer and Salovey's ability model include emotion identification and management (already described), and emotion utilization and understanding.[19] Brackett and Katulak and Kornacki and Caruso described interventions designed to target all of these components. Outcome research is presented in both chapters, and appears promising, but further outcome research focused on these specific techniques would be of interest.

☐ Conclusions

It is clear that the different intervention packages have ingredients that help people. Prior research in psychotherapeutic techniques, coupled with program-specific research evidence presented in this book, suggests that social and emotional learning programs can improve emotional well-being, social effectiveness, social connectedness, and managerial effectiveness. That said, it is not yet clear which ingredients are most essential, which ingredients are inactive or even harmful, and which ingredients are not yet sufficiently included in each intervention. This criticism could, of course, be leveled at most psychological intervention programs. Despite considerable advances in outcome research, much needs to be done. Future research will need to evaluate the efficacy of different ingredients, compared to a placebo condition. This will allow us to gradually build up a set of empirically supported processes that help to reduce human suffering and improve effectiveness.

That said, the programs described here are among the best we have seen in the field. They are theoretically coherent, carefully designed, and follow best practices as presently understood. They appear to be well-accepted by those who have gone through them, and rated as useful. They represent, in other words, some innovative and promising interventions for emotional and personality growth.

☐ References

1. Mayer, J. D., & Salovey, P. (1997). What is emotional intelligence? In P. Salovey & D. J. Sluyter (Eds.), *Emotional development and emotional intelligence: Educational implications* (pp. 3–34). New York: Basic Books.
2. Rosen, G. M., & Davison, G. C. (2003). Psychology should list empirically supported principles of change (ESPs) and not credential trademarked therapies or other treatment packages. *Behavior Modification, 27,* 300–312.
3. Mayer, J. D. (2004). How does psychotherapy influence personality? A theoretical integration. *Journal of Clinical Psychology, 60,* 1291–1315.
4. Mayer, J. D. (2005). A tale of two visions: Can a new view of personality help integrate psychology? *American Psychologist, 60,* 294–307.
5. Elias, M. J. (2006). The connection between academic and social and emotional learning. In M. J. Elias & H. Arnold (Eds.), *The educator's guide to emotional intelligence and academic achievement* (pp. 4–14). Thousand Oaks, CA: Corwin Press.
6. Hayes, S. C., Strosahl, K. D., & Wilson, K. G. (1999). *Acceptance and commitment therapy: An experiential approach to behavior change,* New York: Guilford Press.
7. Zins, J. E., Bloodworth, M., Weissberg, R. P., & Walberg, H. J. (2004). The scientific base linking social and emotional learning to school success. In J. E. Zins, R. P. Weissberg, M. C. Wang, & H. J. Walberg (Eds.), *Building academic success on social and emotional learning: What does the research say?* (pp. 3–22). New York: Teachers College Press.
8. Taylor, G. J. (2000). Recent developments in alexithymia theory and research. *Canadian Journal of Psychiatry, 45,* 134–142.
9. Ciarrochi, J., Scott, G., Deane, F. P., & Heaven, P. C. L. (2003). Relations between social and emotional competence and mental health: A construct validation study. *Personality and Individual Differences, 35,* 1947–1963.
10. Lopes, P. N., Brackett, M. A., Nezlek, J. B., Schutz, A., Sellin, I., & Salovey, P. (2004). Emotional intelligence and social interaction. *Personality and Social Psychology Bulletin, 30,* 1018–1034.
11. Cormier, L. S., & Cormier, W. H. (1998). *Interviewing strategies for helpers: Fundamental skills and cognitive behavioral interventions.* Pacific Grove, CA: Brooks/Cole.

12. Jacobson, N. S., Dobson, K. S., Traux, P., Addis, M. E., Kaerner, K., Gollen, J., Gortner, E., & Prince, S. (1996). A component analysis of cognitive-behavioral treatment for depression. *Journal of Consulting and Clinical Psychology, 64*, 295–304.

13. Masuda, A., Hayes, S., Sackett, C. F., & Twohig, M. P. (2004). Cognitive defusion and self-relevant negative thoughts: Examining the impact of a ninety year old technique. *Behavior Research and Therapy, 42*, 477–485.

14. Hayes, S., Masuda, A., Bisset, R., Luoma, J., & Guerrelo, L. F. (2004). DBT, FAP, and ACT: How empirically oriented are the new behavior therapy technologies? *Behavior Therapy, 35*, 35–54.

15. Bond, F. W., & Bunce, D. (2000). Mediators of change in emotion-focused and problem-focused worksite stress management interventions. *Journal of Occupational Health Psychology, 5*, 156–163.

16. Carter, M., & Barlow, D. H. (1993). Interoceptive exposure in the treatment of panic disorder. In L. VandeCreek, S. Knapp, & T. L. Jackson (Eds.), *Innovations in clinical practice: A source book, Vol. 12* (pp. 329–336). Sarasota, FL: Professional Resource Press.

17. Csikszentmihalyi, M. (1999). If we are so rich, why aren't we happy? *American Psychologist, 54*, 821–827.

18. Sheldon, K. M., & Kasser, T. (2001). Getting older, getting better? Personal strivings and psychological maturity across the life span. *Developmental Psychology, 37*, 491–501.

19. Mayer, J. D., Salovey, P., & Caruso, D. R. (2004). Emotional intelligence: Theory, findings, and implications. *Psychological Inquiry, 15*, 197–215.

AUTHOR INDEX

Ackerman, B., 5
Addis, M. E., 153
Adler, M., 31, 38, 56
Agostin, R. M., 5
Akrivou-Napersky, K., 37, 39
Allen, K. B., 113
Alster, B., 2
American Psychiatric Association, 89
Andersen, S. M., 125, 131
Atkinson, J. W., 128
Auerbach-Major, S., 5
Azim, H. F., 136

Baer, R. A., 113
Bain, S. K., 5
Baldwin, T., 32
Ballou, R., 32, 49
Banyard, V. I., 125
Bar-On, R., 2, 3
Barlow, D. H., 31, 154
Barnes-Holmes, D., 91, 93, 95,
    119
Barnes-Holmes, Y., 119
Bartholemew, K., 125
Bayliss, V., xiv, 89, 144
Beaubien, J. M., 44
Bechara, A., 54
Beck, A. T., 130
Beck, J. S., 97
Bellak, L., 127
Bennis, W., 35, 37
Berk, M. S., 125
Berlew, D. E., 33, 37
Bilich, L., xiv, 89, 144
Bishop, S., 94
Bissett, R., 94, 96, 153
Black, B., 133
Blackledge, J., xiv, 89, 100, 118, 144
Blair, K. A., 5
Blaize, N., 37, 38
Block, J., 96
Bloodworth, M., 151

Boesky, D., 127
Bond, F. W., 96, 154
Bosco, J. S., 3
Bowers, D., 32, 49
Bowers, K. S., 134
Boyatzis, R. E., xiii, xiv, 28, 29, 30, 31, 32,
    33, 34, 35, 37, 38, 39, 43, 44, 48, 49, 144,
    145, 147, 148, 151, 152
Brackett, M. A., xiii, 1, 2, 3, 4, 5, 6, 15, 23,
    24, 119, 120, 144, 145, 146, 147, 152,
    153, 154
Bradshaw, D., 38
Bradway, K. P., 138
Brenner, C., 127
Brown, K. W., 113
Brownstein, A. J., 93
Bunce, D., 96, 154
Burke, M. J., 32
Byham, W. C., 30

Campbell, J. P., 31
Cantor, N., 131
Caputi, P., 119
Carpenter, M., 24
Carter, M., 154
Caruso, D. R., xiii, xiv, 1, 3, 5, 6, 53, 55, 56,
    119, 120, 144, 145, 146, 147, 148, 152,
    154
Chan, A. Y. C., 119
Cheeseman Day, J., 132
Chen, G., 44
Cherniss, C., 31, 38, 56
Ciarrochi, J., xiv, 56, 89, 97, 100, 114, 118,
    119, 120, 144, 145, 147, 148, 149, 150,
    151, 153
Clift, R. J., 5
Colby, S. M., 94
Colder, M., 94
Cooper, C. L., 4
Copper, J. T., 2
Cormier, L. S., 153
Cormier, W. H., 153

157

Costa, P. T., Jr., 127
Côté, S., 4
Cowan, K., 56
Cox, W. M., 135
Coyne, L. W., 100
Cravens, R. B., 138
Crick, N., 5
Crombez, G., 94
Cronbach, L. J., 127
Csikszentmihalyi, M., 89, 154
Custrini, R. J., 4

Dahl, J., 97
Damasio, A. R., 54
Darling-Hammond, L., 4, 5
Davidson, R. J., 94
Davison, G. C., 145
Day, R. R., 32
Deane, F. P., 114, 153
DeMulder, E., 5
Denham, S. A., 4, 5
Dennett, D. C., 134
Development Dimensions International
  (DDI), 32
Dixon, N. M., 32
Dobson, K. S., 153
Dodge, K. A., 5
Dornheim, L., 2
Dreyfus, C., 48
Dugas, D. M., 94
Duncan, B. L., 31
Dunnette, M. D., 31
Dunsmore, J. C., 4
Durlak, J. A., 1
Dutton, D. G., 5

Eifert, G., 94
Eisenberg, N., 4
Elias, M., 1, 2, 3, 24, 146, 151
Ellis, A., 97
Emery, G., 130
Emmerling, R., 56
Epstein, S., 138
Erber, R., 94

Fabes, R. A., 4
Fale, E., 2
Feldman, R. S., 4
Feldner, M., 94
Fine, S., 5
Fisher, G., 94, 96
Fong, C. T., 35, 37
Ford, J. K., 32
Forgas, J. P., 119, 120
Forman, E. M., 139
Fox, E., 93
Fredericks, L., 1, 3

Fredrickson, B. L., 136
Frederickson, N., 119, 120
Freeston, M. H., 94
Frey, K., 1, 2, 24
Fuller, M., 138
Funder, D. C., 138
Furnham, A., 2, 119, 120

Gagnon, F., 94
Gall, M., 4
Gediman, H., 127
Geher, G., 3, 119, 120
Gibson, L. E., 125
Gifford, E. V., 93
Gil-Olarte Márquez, P., 4
Godsell, C., 97
Goldberg, L. R., 127
Golden, C. J., 2
Goldstein, A. P., 31
Goleman, D., 30, 33, 39, 42, 56
Gollen, J., 153
Gortner, E., 153
Gotlib, I. H., 5
Greenberg, T., 1, 2, 3, 5, 24
Greenwald, A. G., 132
Greenway, D. E., 93
Gregg, J., 96
Grencavage, L. M. N., 139
Grewal, D., 4
Gross, J. J., 5
Guerrelo, L. F., 153
Gully, S. M., 44

Haas, J. R., 93
Haggerty, D. J., 2
Hahn, T. N., 109
Hakel, M. D., 56
Halberstadt, A. G., 4
Hall, L. E., 2
Halpern, D. F., 56
Hand, H. H., 32
Hansen, N. B., 139
Hargreaves, A., 4
Harvey, A. G., 94
Hayes, S. C., 89, 91, 93, 94, 95, 96, 100,
  109, 110, 115, 119, 145, 149, 150, 151,
  153, 154
Haynes, N., 1, 2, 24
Hazen, N. L., 133
Healy, O., 93
Heaven, P. C. L., 114, 153
Heidenreich, T., 135
Helson, R., 126
Hilgard, E. R., 127
Hodges, S. D., 54
Hodgetts, R. M., 30
Horowitz, L. M., 125

Howard, K. I., 139
Hoyer, J., 135
Hubble, M. A., 31
Hurvich, M., 127

Izard, C., 5

Jacobson, N. S., 153
Jarrett, M. Q., 31, 32
John, C., 139
Johnson, C. A., 5
Johnston, S., 94
Joyce, A. S., 136

Kabat-Zinn, J., 109, 110
Kadis, J., 4
Kaerner, K., 153
Kanfer, F. H., 31
Kapleau, P., 109
Kasch, K. L., 5
Kasser, T., 154
Katulak, N. A., xiii, 2, 144, 145, 146, 147, 152, 154
Kelly, G. A., 131
Kendall, P. C., 5
Kessler, R., 1, 2, 24
Kihlstrom, J. F., 134
Kilcullen, R. N., 44
Klinger, E., 135
Kohlenberg, B. S., 94, 96
Kolb, D. A., 32, 33, 37, 38, 44, 48, 49
Kopta, M. S., 139
Kornacki, S. A., xiv, 53, 144, 145, 146, 147, 148, 152, 154
Koster, E. H. W., 94
Kotter, J. P., 30
Kram, K. E., 49
Krause, M. S., 139
Kremenitzer, J. P., 24

Ladouceur, R., 94
Lambert, M. J., 139
Latham, G. P., 32, 44
Lawler, E. E. III, 31
Leitenberg, H., 125
Leonard, D., 44
Leong, F. T. L., 139
Lerner, N., 3, 4
Levitas, J., 5
Lillis, J., 96
Lisle, D. J., 54
Littledyke, M., 138
Locke, E. A., 44
Lopes, P. N., 3, 4, 56, 153
Losada, M. F., 136
Luoma, J., 96, 153
Luthans, F., 30

McCallum, M., 136
McClelland, D. C., 30, 37, 128
McCrae, R. R., 127
McKee, A., 30, 33, 37, 38, 43
McKibbin, L., 35, 37
MacLean, P. D., 128
Malouff, J. M., 2
Masuda, A., 96, 153
Matthews, G., 2
Maurer, M., 15
Mayer, J. D., xiii, xiv, 1, 2, 3, 4, 55, 56, 119, 120, 125, 127, 128, 131, 133, 135, 144, 145, 154
Meehl, P. E., 127
Meichenbaum, D., 97
Memeroff, W. F., 32
Michalak, J., 135
Miller, S. D., 31
Mintzberg, H., 35, 37
Mischel, W., 131, 138
Monti, P. M., 94
Morris, A. S., 5
Morrow, C. C., 31, 32
Mostow, A., 5

Naring, G. W. B., 94
Neuberger, E. C., 132
Nellum-Williams, R., 5
Nezlek, J. B., 3, 153
Nilsson, A., 97
No Child Left Behind Act of 2001 (NCLB), 2, 14
Noe, R. A., 32
Novy, P. L., 125

O'Brien, M. U., 1, 3
O'Neil, R., 5
O'Toole, J., 35, 37
Ogrodniczuk, J. S., 136
Olweus, D., 138
Omori, M., 4
Orlinsky, D. E., 139
Ornstein, R., 134

Padilla, M., 94, 96
Palfai, T. P., 94
Palomera Martín, R., 4
Parke, R. D., 5
Pascarella, E. T., 31
Payne, S. C., 44
Pennebaker, J. W., 94
Peterson, B. E., 125, 126
Petrides, K. V., 2, 119, 120
Pfeffer, L., 35, 37
Philippot, P., 4
Pinker, S., 134
Piper, W. E., 136

Plutchik, R., 74
Porter, L., 35, 37
Pribram, K. H., 134
Primrose, A. F., 138
Prince, S., 153

Queenan, P., 5

Rapp, H. C., 131
Rassin, E., 94
Renio-McKee, A., 32
Resnik, H., 1, 3
Reynolds, D., 5
Richards, M. D., 32
Rivers, S., 3, 4, 23
Robb, H., 97, 119
Roberts, R. D., 2
Roche, B., 91, 95, 119
Roget, N., 94, 96
Rohsensow, D. J., 94
Rosen, G. M., 145
Rosete, D., 56
Rosenkrantz, S. A., 30
Rottenberg, J., 5
Rouse, D., 94
Rubin, M. M., 5
Rupinski, M. T., 31, 32
Rush, A. J., 130
Ryan, R. M., 113

Saari, L. M., 32
Saarni, C., 4, 5, 120
Sackett, C. F., 153
Salovey, P., xiii, 1, 2, 3, 4, 5, 23, 55, 56, 119,
    120, 128, 145, 153, 154
Sandlin, P., 33
Sawyer, K., 5
Schmitt, N., 32
Schooler, J. W., 54
Schultz, D., 5
Schutte, N. S., 2
Schutz, A., 3, 153
Schwabstone, M., 1, 2, 24
Schwartz, G. E., 94
Scott, G., 114, 153
Segal, Z. V., 109
Sellin, I., 3, 153
Shapiro, D., 132
Sharp, L. K., 94
Shaw, B. F., 130
Sheldon, K. M., 154
Shiffman, S., 3, 4
Shipman, K., 5
Shriver, T., 1, 2, 24
Siegal, J. A., 125
Silk, J. S., 5
Singer, L. J., 131

Sitarenios, G., 119
Slocum, J. W. Jr., 32
Slutyer, D. J., 5
Smith, C. P., 128
Smith, G. T., 113
Smith, M., 37, 38
Sokol, M., 32
Southam-Gerow, M. A., 5
Specht, L., 33
Spencer, L. M., Jr., 30
Spencer, S. M., 30
Spira, A., 94
Srivastava, S., 126
Steinberg, L., 5
Strand, C., 5
Strauss, R., 56
Strosahl, K. D., 89, 93, 95, 96, 100,
    109, 110, 115, 145, 149, 150, 151,
    154
Stubbs, E. C., 31, 32
Sullivan, M. L. L., 94
Sutton, R. E., 1, 4
Suveg, C., 5

Taylor, G. J., 114, 153
Taylor, S. N., 31, 32
Teasedale, J. D., 109
Tedlie, C., 5
Terenzini, P. T., 31
Thompson, C. W., 138
Thompson, L., 32
Thornton, G. C., 30
Tomkins, S. S., 128
Tranel, D., 54
Traux, P., 153
Travers, C. J., 4
Trinidad, D. R., 5
Twohig, M. P., 153

Veroff, J., 128

Walberg, H. J., 1, 2, 5
Wang, M. C., 1, 2, 5
Wang, S., 5
Warner, R. M., 3, 4
Wegner, D. M., 94
Weick, K. E., 31
Weinberger, D. A., 94
Weiner, I. B., 136
Weissberg, R. P., 1, 2, 3, 5, 24
Welsh, M., 5
Wentworth, P., 125, 126
Wenzlaff, R. M., 94
Wexley, K. N., 32
Wheatley, K. F., 1, 4
Wheeler, J. V., 32, 49
Whiteman, J. A., 44

Wilde, Oscar, 56
Williams, J. M. G., 109
Williams, L. M., 125, 131
Wilson, K. G., 89, 93, 95, 96, 97, 100, 109,
  110, 115, 145, 149, 150, 151, 154
Wilson, T. D., 54
Winter, S. K., 33, 37
Winters, J., 5
Woolfe, C. J., 2
Wulf, R., 135

Young, D. P., 32
Youngstrom, E., 5

Zachar, P., 139
Zanakos, S., 94
Zeidner, M., 2
Zeman, J., 5
Zins, J., 1, 2, 3, 5, 24,
  151
Zvolensky, M., 94

SUBJECT INDEX

Page entries for main headings which also have subheadings refer only to general aspects of that topic.

Page entries in **bold** refer to figures/tables.

ABC worksheet, 108, 120
Ability-based EI development, xiv, 55–58; *see also* Emotional blueprint
  assessment of EI ability, 56
  decision making, 54
  defining EI, 55
  development exercises, *see below*
  evaluation/follow-up, 57
  guided experience, 56–57
  gut feelings, 66, 67
  intelligent use of emotions, 53–54
  interpersonal EI, 55
  intrapersonal EI, 55
  Mayer-Salovey-Caruso EI Test (MSCEIT) assessment of improvement, 57–58, **58**
  on-going support/refresher training, 57
  payoffs/advantages of using EI, 55–56
  performance enhancement, 56
  relevance to real world, 57
  unconscious emotions, 54
Ability-based EI development exercises
  1: learning styles and payoffs, 58–59
  2: basic emotional self-awareness, 60–62, **61**
  3: what does EI behavior look like, 62–66
  4: Emotional blueprint case study, 66–69
  5: emotional experiences, 69–71
  6: feelings and emotions, 71–73
  7: energy of emotions, 73–76, **75**
  8: emotional lenses, 76–79, **77**, **78**, **79**
  9: emotional lens personal application, 80–82, **81**, **82**
  10: transforming, influencing, using EI, 82–86

Academic performance, 1, 3–5, 24
Acceptance, *see* Emotional orientation
Acceptance and Commitment Therapy (ACT), 96–97
Action implementation personality system, 127, **130**, 132–133, 136
  and energy development, 133
  improving, 136, 138
  malfunction, **140**
Action orientation, **98**, 115–119
  compass metaphor, 117
  definition, 115
  exercise 1: funeral exercise, 116
  exercise 2: values/goals distinction, 117, **118**
  exercise 3: value clarification, 118–119
  friendship example, 119
  promoting value congruent behavior, 120
  values, clarifying, 115, 118–119
  visual metaphor, **116**
Actualization, self, 137
Adlerian therapy, 136
Advertising, 18–19, **19**
Aggressiveness, long-term changes in, 138
Alcohol use, 114
Anxiety, 4, 5
  ACT for, 96
  management, 4–5
Associations, feeling words, 15
Avoidance behaviors, *see* Emotional orientation; Experiential avoidance
Awareness, emotional, *see* Identifying emotions; Understanding emotions; *see also* Emotional blueprint

Basic urges/motivations, 128, 130;
  see also Energy development
Bias/distortion, mental models, 132
Big Five trait approach, 127
Boiling frog metaphor, 37–38, 42–43

CASEL (Collaborative for Academic, Social
  and Emotional Learning), 1, 2
CBT, 97, 119, 153
Change, *see* Discontinuities; Intentional
  change theory; Personality change
Circumplex model of emotions, **75**
Cognitive behavioral therapy, *see* CBT
Cognitive fusion, 91, 101
Cognitive restructuring, 153
Collaborative for Academic, Social and
  Emotional Learning (CASEL), 1, 2
Comparison of EI interventions, *see*
  Interventions (comparison)
Compass metaphor, 117
Competencies, developing EI, xiv, 29–30,
  49–50; *see also* Intervention
  techniques; Leadership Executive
  Assessment and Development Course
  alternative manifestations of, 30
  definition of competencies, 29
  experiential learning theory, 38
  growth/development of, 31–33;
    see also Discontinuities (change)
  honeymoon effect, 31
  intentional change theory, xiv, 33–35,
    34, **36**, 38
  relationship-management cluster, 30
  results of standard training programs,
    32–33, **33**
  self-awareness cluster, 30
  self-management cluster, 30
  social awareness cluster, 30
Conscious self-regulation, *see* Executive
  control
Consortium on Research on Emotional
  Intelligence in Organizations, 31
Consumer advertising, 18–19, **19**
Control, self, *see* Executive control

Decision making, using rationality and
  emotion, 54
Defense mechanisms, 42, 43
  interpreting, 136
Definitions
  action orientation, 115
  change techniques, 135
  competencies, 29
  EI, 55, 90, 119
  EIB, 90
  personality, 126
  values, 115

Defusing words, *see* Language (defusion)
Depression, 4, 5
  ACT for, 96
  and mental energy system malfunctions,
    130, 139, **140**
Developing EI competencies,
  see Competencies, EI; *see also* Ability-
  based EI development
Discontinuities of change, 35
  boiling frog analogy/self-image, 37–38,
    42–43
  case studies, 40–42
  catching dreams/engaging passion, 37,
    38–39
  defense mechanisms, 42, 43
  feeling safe/secure, 48
  goal-setting, 44
  Ideal Self/personal vision, 37, 38–39,
    40–42, 49
  learning agenda, mindfulness through,
    38, 41, 43–44, 48
  learning plan examples, 44–47
  metamorphosis, 47–48
  performance orientation, 44
  Real Self, 43, 49
  relationships that facilitate learning,
    48–49
  self-confidence, 49
  team building/group management, 48
  trusting ability to change, 49
Distortion, mental models, 132
Dream catching, 37, 38–39
Drug use, 4, 5, 114

EI, *see* Emotional intelligence; Emotionally
  intelligent behavior
ELMS, *see* Emotional Literacy in the Middle
  School program
Emergences/discontinuities of change,
  see Discontinuities
Emotional awareness, *see* Identifying
  emotions; Understanding emotions;
  see also Emotional
  blueprint
Emotional blueprint, xiv, 2–6, 23, 55;
  see also Emotional intelligence
  interventions; Identifying emotions;
  Managing emotions; Understanding
  emotions; Using emotions
  case study, 66–69
  exercises, 63–64
Emotional intelligence (EI), 2–5
  definition, 90, 119
  inter/intrapersonal, 55
  interventions, *see* Competencies;
  Emotional Literacy in the Middle
  School program; Emotionally

Intelligent Teacher workshop;
Interventions (comparing); Leadership
Executive Assessment and
Development Course; Mindfulness-
based emotional intelligence training;
Personality changes; School-based
interventions
skill-based model, *see* Emotional
blueprint; *see also* Identifying emotions;
Managing emotions; Understanding
emotions; Using emotions
tests, 3, 57–58, **58**
theory, 2, 3, 145, 146
training, practical approach, 53–54,
86–87; *see also* Ability-based EI
development
Emotional lenses, *see* Lenses, emotional
Emotional Literacy in the Middle School
(ELMS) program, 2, 14–23, 24
feeling words, 14, 15
management of emotion, 19–20, 20–22,
21, **22**
mass media advertising, 18–19, **19**
perception/expression of emotion, 17, **18**
quality assurance, 22–23
student activities, 16
understanding emotion, 20
use of emotion, 18–20
Emotional management, *see* Managing
emotions; *see also* Emotional blueprint;
Using emotions
Emotional orientation, 97–101, **98**, 114,
149, 154; *see also* Experiential
avoidance
exercise 1: discovering pervasiveness of
avoidance, 99–100
exercise 2: lie detector, 100–101
rules of public/private experience, 101
Emotional understanding, *see*
Understanding emotions;
see also Emotional blueprint
Emotionally intelligent behavior (EIB)
definition, 90
examples, 63–65
increasing, 97
role in reducing suffering/unhappiness,
91
The Emotionally Intelligent Teacher (EIT)
workshop, 2, 5–14, 23
EI blueprint, 5–6, 23
management of emotion, 5, 6, 11–13, **12**,
13
perception/expression of emotion, 5, 6,
7, **8**
quality assurance, 13–14
stress coping mechanisms, 5
teacher activities, 6–7

understanding emotion, 5, 6, 9–11, **10**
use of emotion, 5, 6, 8–9
Empathy, 23
learning plan to improve, 44–46
Empty-chair technique, 135
Energy development personality system,
127, 128–130, **129**, 133
basic urges/motivations, 128, 130
improving, 135, 137
malfunctions, 130, 139, **140**
Energy of emotions, 73–76
circumplex model of emotions, **75**
EI skill development, understanding
emotions, 73
rules governing emotions, 74
Entailment, mutual/combinatorial, 92, 94
Evaluating emotions, *see* Identifying
emotions; Understanding emotions
Evidence-base, EI interventions, 1–2, 145,
152–154
Executive control system, 127, **130**,
133–134
improving, 136, 138
and other functions, 134
malfunction, 139, **140**
Experience
emotional, development exercises,
69–71
guided, 56–57
public/private, 101, 109–110
Experiential avoidance, 93–94, 96;
see also Emotional orientation
association with psychopathology,
94
contextual control, 96
suppression strategies, 94
Experiential learning theory, 38
Exposure techniques/systematic
desensitization, 135, 154
Expression of emotion, *see* Identifying
emotions; *see also* Emotional blueprint

Feeling/s; *see also* Emotion/al
and emotions, 71–73
words, 14, 15, 16
Four-branch model, *see* Emotional
blueprint; Identifying emotions;
Managing emotions;
Understanding emotions; Using
emotions
Friendship example, 119
Functional contextualism, 119, 120
Funeral exercise, 116
Fusion, cognitive, 91, 101

Gestalt therapy, 135
Group management, 48

Guided experience, 56–57
Gut feelings, 66, 67

Happiness, human, 89–90, 91, 96
Health, physical, 5
Hope, 135
Hyperactivity, 4, 5, 24

Ideal Self/personal vision, 37, 38–39,
    40–42, 49
  case studies, 40–42
  and Real Self, 43, 49
Identifying emotions, 2–3, **98**, 146–147,
    153; *see also* Emotional blueprint;
    Understanding emotions
  development exercises, 60–62, 62–63
  EIT workshop, 5, 6, 7, **8**
  ELMS program, 17, **18**
  misinterpretations of others, 5, 56
  mood meter, 61/**61**
  non-analytic/non-reasoning techniques,
    113
  tin can monster metaphor, 114–115
  unconscious emotions, 54
Impulsivity, 139, **140**
Influencing others, 82, 83, 85, 86
  example, 84–85
Intelligence, emotional, *see* Emotional
    intelligence
Intelligence Quotient (IQ), changes in,
    138
Intentional change theory, xiv, 33–35, **34**,
    36, 38, 145
Interpersonal EI, 55
Interpersonal relationships, *see*
    Relationships
Interventions (EI), comparing, xiii, xiv–xv,
    144, 145–146, 154–155; *see also*
    Emotional intelligence interventions
  defusion of language, 150, 153
  emotional orientation, 149, 154
  empirical/evidence base, 1–2, 145,
    152–154
  identifying emotions, 146–147, 153
  increasing ethical/prosocial behavior,
    151
  intentional change theory, 145
  knowledge of effective/ineffective
    behaviors, 151–152
  language processes/experiential
    avoidance, 145
  managing emotions, 148, 149, 153
  mindfulness-based approaches, xiv,
    147–151
  positive personality change, xiv, 148–149
  theory/theoretical comparison, 145, 146
  understanding emotions, 147–148, 154

using emotions to facilitate thought, 147,
    154
  value clarification, 151, 154
Intrapersonal EI, 55
IQ, changes in, 138

Key life discoveries, *see* Competencies,
    developing EI; Leadership Executive
    Assessment and Development (LEAD)
    Course; Ideal Self
Knowledge guidance personality system,
    127, **129**, 130–132; *see also* Mental
    models/representations
  improving, 136, 137
  malfunction, **140**

Language
  contextual control of processes (principle
    4), 95–96
  defusion of, *see below*
  derivations, 92–93, 95
  dominance of processes (principle 2),
    92–93
  as experience changing (principle 1),
    91–92
  experiential avoidance (principle 3),
    93–94, 96
  and human happiness, 89–90, 91, 96
  and human progress, 89–90
Language defusion, **98**, 101–113, 150, 153
  ABC worksheet, 108, 120
  defusion strategies/refusing to believe
    unhelpful rules/evaluations, 101–102,
    102, **103**
  exercise 1: distinctions between
    descriptions, evaluations and rules,
    103–7, **106**, **107**
  exercise 2: making words lose their
    power over us, 107–108
  exercise 3: looking at thoughts rather
    than through them, 108
  exercise 4: becoming mindful of private
    experiences, 109–110
  exercise 5: facilitating observer
    perspective, 110–113, **111**, **112**, **113**
  self as context, 110, **111**
  Zen Buddhist mindfulness practice,
    109–110
Leadership Executive Assessment and
    Development (LEAD) Course, 35–38,
    36
  course evaluations, 38, **39**
  impact/outcomes, 37–38
  learning agenda/plan, 38, 41
  motivation and drive, 31
  overall objectives, 36–37
  personal balance sheet, 37–38

personal vision, 37
resonant relationships/mutual caring,
    37, 38
tipping points, 37, 42
Learning style emotional ability exercise,
    58–59
Lenses, emotional, 76–79, **77**, **78**
    personal application exercises, 80–82, **81**,
    82

Maladaptive behavior, 4, 5, 24
Managing emotions, xiv, 2–6; *see also*
    Emotional blueprint; Using emotions
    anxiety management, 4–5
    critique/evaluation, 120, 148, 149, 153
    development exercises, 62–63, 66–67,
        76–77, 80, 82–83
    EIT workshop, 5, 6, 11–13, **12**, **13**
    ELMS program, 19–20, 20–22, **21**, **22**
Mass media advertising, 18–19, **19**
Mayer-Salovey-Caruso Emotional
    Intelligence Tests (MSCEIT/MSCEIT-
    YV), 3, 57–58, **58**
MBEIT, *see* Mindfulness-based emotional
    intelligence training
Mental energy system, *see* Energy
    development
Mental models/representations, 131–132
    benefits of good, 132
    biased/distorted, 132
    improving, 137–138
    incomplete, 131–132
Metaphors
    boiling frog, 37–38, 42–43
    compass, 117
    tin can monster, 114–115
    use of, 97
    visual, **116**
Mindfulness-based emotional intelligence
    training (MBEIT), xiv, 89–90,
    119–120, 134; *see also* Experiential
    avoidance; Language; Relational frame
    theory
    Acceptance and Commitment Therapy
        (ACT), 96–97
    action orientation, 115
    bringing EI dimensions together exercise,
        119
    and cognitive behavior therapy, 97, 119
    cognitive fusion, 91, 101
    comparison with other
        interventions/critique, 147–151
    definitions, 90–91
    dimensions, *see* Action orientation;
        Emotional awareness; Emotional
        orientation; Language defusion
    emotional intelligence (EI), 90, 119

emotionally intelligent behavior (EIB),
    90
    evidence for, 96–97
    functional contextualism, 119, 120
    increasing EIB, 97
    through learning agenda, 38, 41, 43–44,
        48
    managing emotions, 120
    metaphor use, 97
    personal experience as guide, 97
    psychological illness, prevalence of, 89
    reason giving, 95
    values, 115
    willingness and commitment worksheet,
        119, 121
Models, mental, *see* Mental
    models/representations
Mood meter, 61/**61**
Motivations, 128, 130; *see also* Energy
    development
MSCEIT/MSCEIT-YV (Mayer-Salovey-
    Caruso Emotional Intelligence Tests),
    3, 57–58, **58**

Observer perspective, 110–113, **111**, **112**,
    113
Oughts/musts, 101

Paranoia, 132
Perception, emotional, *see* Identifying
    emotions; *see also* Emotional blueprint
Performance enhancement, 56
Personal vision, *see* Ideal Self/personal
    vision
Personality change, positive, xiv, 125–127,
    139–140, **140**, 148–149; *see also*
    Psychotherapy
    actualization, 137
    case study, 125–126, 137
    goals, **140**
    gradual nature of, 48, 138–139, 140
    improving personality system, 136–138
    pathways, 134
    targeting specific personality systems,
        137
Personality function/structure, 127–134
    Big Five trait approach, 127
    definition of personality, 126
    malfunctions, 130, 132, 139, **140**
    stock-taking, 126
    structural approach, xv, 127
    systems set, 127, **129–130**; *see also* Action
        implementation; Energy development;
        Executive control; Knowledge
        guidance; Mental
        models/representations
    types, 127

Phobias, 135
Post-traumatic stress disorder, 149
Practical approach to EI training, 53–54,
   86–87; *see also* Ability-based EI
   development
Private experience, 101
   becoming mindful of, 109–110
Progress, human, 89–90
Psychodrama, 135
Psychodynamic therapy, 136
Psychological illness/psychopathology, 89,
   94, 132, 135, 149; *see also* Anxiety;
   Depression; Personality malfunction
Psychotherapy, 134, 138–139
   targeting specific personality systems,
   135–136
PTSD (Post-traumatic stress disorder),
   149
Public experience, 101

Real Self, 43, 49
Reason giving, 95
Reasoning, inductive/deductive, 8
   non-analytic/non-reasoning techniques,
   113
Reference groups, 48
Reframing technique, 136
Relational frame theory (RFT), 91, 92
   mutual/combinatorial entailment, 92, 94
   transformation of stimulus functions, 92,
   93, 95, 96
Relationships, 1, 3, 4, 5
   facilitating learning, 48–49
   resonant, 37, 38
   therapeutic, 135
Representations mental, *see* Mental
   models/representations
Revelations, 35; *see also* Discontinuities
RFT, *see* Relational frame theory
Rules
   governing emotions, 74
   unhelpful, *see* Language (defusion)

School-based interventions, xiii, 1–2,
   23–24; *see also* Emotional Literacy in
   the Middle School program; The
   Emotionally Intelligent Teacher
   workshop
   academic performance, 1, 3–5, 24
   anxiety management, 4–5
   emotional intelligence, 2–5
   evidence-basis for, 1–2
   implementation, US schools, 24
   interpersonal relationships/social
   competence, 1, 3, 4, 5
   maladaptive behavior, 4, 5, 24
   managing emotions, 2–6

Mayer-Salovey-Caruso Emotional
   Intelligence Tests, 3–5
   perception/expression of emotion, 2, 3,
   5, 6
   skill-based model, 2–3
   teacher stress/burnout, 4
   understanding emotion, 2, 3, 5, 6
   use of emotion, 2, 3, 5, 6
Self
   actualization, 137
   Ideal, *see* Ideal Self/personal vision
   image, 42–43
   Real, 43, 49
   regulation, *see* Executive control
Skill-based model, *see* Emotional blueprint;
   see also Identifying emotions;
   Managing emotions; Understanding
   emotions; Using emotions
Social competence, 1, 3, 4, 5
Speech anxiety, Acceptance and
   Commitment Therapy, 96
Stimulus functions, transformation, 92, 93,
   95, 96
Stress reduction; *see also* Post-traumatic
   stress disorder
   Acceptance and Commitment Therapy,
   96
   coping mechanisms, 5
   teacher, 4, 6–7
Suppression strategies, 94
Systematic desensitization, 135, 154

Teachers/teaching, *see* Emotional Literacy
   in the Middle School; The Emotionally
   Intelligent Teacher workshop;
   School-based interventions
Team building/group management, 48
Therapeutic relationship, 135
Thought suppression strategies, 94
Tin can monster metaphor, 114–115
Trait approach, personality, 127
Transference, interpreting, 136
Transformation of stimulus functions, 92,
   93, 95, 96

Unconscious emotions, 54, 136; *see also*
   Emotional blueprint; Identifying
   emotions; Understanding emotions
Understanding emotions, 2, 3, 147–148,
   154; *see also* Emotional blueprint
   development exercises, 62–63, 66–67,
   71, 73
   EIT workshop, 5, 6, 9–11, **10**
   ELMS program, 20
Using emotions, 2, 3, 147, 154; *see also*
   Emotional blueprint; Managing
   emotions

development exercises, 62–63, 66–67,
  69–70, 71, 82–83
EIT workshop, 5, 6, 8–9
ELMS program, 18–20
manipulation of own emotions, 19–20
mass media advertising, 18–19, **19**
Urges/motivations, 128, 130; *see also*
  Energy development

Values
  and congruent behavior, 120
  clarifying, xiv, 115, 151, 154
  definition, 115
  exercise 3:, 118–119
  friendship example, 119

goals distinction, 117, **118**
Violence, 5
Vision, personal, *see* Ideal Self/personal
  vision
Visual metaphor, **116**

Weatherhead School of Management, 32,
  35, 38
Willingness and commitment worksheet,
  119, 121
Words, power of, *see* Language
Workplace outcomes, 4

Zen Buddhist mindfulness practice,
  109–110